ROMANCE
OF THE NATIONAL PARKS

Photograph—Department of the Interior

Courtesy—Portfolio, American Planning and Civic Association

MARIPOSA GROVE OF REDWOODS IN YOSEMITE

ROMANCE
OF THE NATIONAL PARKS

BY

HARLEAN JAMES

EXECUTIVE SECRETARY, AMERICAN PLANNING AND CIVIC ASSOCIATION

NEW YORK
THE MACMILLAN COMPANY
1939

PRINTED IN UNITED STATES OF AMERICA

Mount Pleasant Press
HARRISBURG, PENNSYLVANIA

To

J. HORACE McFARLAND

WHO, AS PRESIDENT OF THE AMERICAN CIVIC ASSOCI-
ATION, ACTIVELY PROMOTED PUBLIC EDUCATION IN
NATIONAL PARK POSSIBILITIES, AND FIRST PROPOSED
A NATIONAL PARK SYSTEM

WHO FOR THIRTY YEARS HAS JOINED IN DEFENDING
THE NATIONAL PARKS AGAINST SELFISH AGGRESSION

AND

WHO HAS NEVER BEEN FOUND WANTING WHEN
THE NATIONAL PARKS NEEDED A FRIEND

FOREWORD

I HAVE had the good fortune to be intimately connected with national parks ever since I first went to Washington in 1913 as a member of the staff of Franklin K. Lane, Secretary of the Interior. I had the privilege of assisting at the birth of the National Park Service, which I served for seventeen years.

Only one who is thoroughly familiar with the inside history of the national parks can appreciate how faithfully Miss James has translated to the public the trend of Congressional legislation during the past sixty years, and the significance of the development of the National Park Service under the guidance and with the support of succeeding Secretaries of the Interior.

We have in national parks today a widely recognized form of land-use which includes recreation, inspiration and education, and which rules out certain conflicting uses appropriate in a multiple-use program applied to other lands. Miss James shows clearly that the National Park System is built upon this recognition.

When I resigned from the Directorship of the National Park Service to enter the business field, I was very glad to accept the invitation of the American Civic Association to become a member of its Executive Board, for I was thoroughly familiar with the active part that Dr. J. Horace McFarland, its President for twenty years, had played in the educational campaign leading to the establishment of the National Park Service. When I was invited in 1937 to become President of the American Planning and Civic Association, to succeed the Honorable Frederic A. Delano, who then became Chairman of the Board, I was proud thus to become the successor of Mr. Delano and Dr. McFarland, and to aid in giving continuing coöperation to the Department of the Interior for the protection of national park ideals and for the defense of national park areas from destructive adverse uses.

For eighteen years, in association with three presidents, Miss James has served the American Civic Association and its successor, the American Planning and Civic Association. During these years millions of American citizens have visited national parks and have become familiar with them. Miss James not only traces the past

FOREWORD

history and present service of national parks and monuments; she looks into the future and shows what may be accomplished to guarantee to this and future generations the effective preservation of adequate national parks which meet the high standards developed by Congress and the Department of the Interior.

Thus, the pages which follow do read as romance to me. I can bear testimony to the accuracy and spirit of what Miss James has written, and I commend to the reading public the perusal of this book on the "Romance of the National Parks."

HORACE M. ALBRIGHT

New York, April, 1939

PREFACE

THE purpose of this book has been to bring together in brief form the history of the movement which led to the creation of national parks and to outline the development of the system. The legislation of Congress and the administration of national parks by the Department of the Interior have contributed to a substantially consistent policy which recognizes national parks as a definite and separate form of land-use.

The space devoted to the different parks and monuments is in no wise a measure of their importance and interest. Certain parks have achieved significance because of the part they have played in the development of the national park idea.

No attempt has been made to present all of the functions of the National Park Service, or to outline all of the additional services rendered during the recent emergency years. Not all of the areas administered by the Service have been mentioned, as the mere catalogue of these is so long that it would make tedious reading. There is, however, on pages 234–5, a map which presents a comprehensive picture of the National Park Service Areas and Projects.

Acknowledgments are made to Dr. Harold C. Bryant, of the National Park Service, for aid in finding source material; to Horace M. Albright, former Director of the Service and now President of the American Planning and Civic Association; to Arno B. Cammerer, Director, Arthur E. Demaray, Associate Director, and George L. Collins, all of the Park Service; to Mrs. Edward R. Padgett, Editor of *Planning and Civic Comment* and to Mrs. Charles W. Williams, of the staff of the American Planning and Civic Association, who read the manuscript and made valuable suggestions; to the many park rangers who all unknowingly and anonymously contributed to the making of this book; to the American Forestry Association, Sierra Club, Appalachian Mountain Club, American Society of Landscape Architects, and the American Planning and Civic Association, all of which organizations furnished plates for the illustrations.

The author is grateful for the opportunity to consult and quote from the John Muir books, the bulletins issued by the National

PREFACE

Park Service, and the many other publications on which she drew heavily in order to bring together the heterogeneous types of material included in the narrative.

It is hoped that those who read the volume may be influenced to visit the parks, and find there inspiration and understanding of the great forces which created them. To become acquainted with the National Park Service field men in the gray-green uniforms is an experience worth remembering. These men are the interpreters of the parks to the public.

If those who visit the national parks and monuments find in this volume the impulse to penetrate beyond the paved highways, and to find in them something of the rest, recreation and knowledge which is there for the taking, the author will feel that in some small measure the book is justified.

But for Dr. J. Horace McFarland this book would never have been written. He suggested the preparation of the manuscript. He helped to make part of the history recorded in it.

HARLEAN JAMES

Washington, D. C., April, 1939

CONTENTS

C O N T E N T S

BOOK II—JOURNEYS

ILLUSTRATIONS

ILLUSTRATIONS

Romance of the National Parks

BOOK I — HISTORY

"NATIONAL PARK" LANGFORD

"There ought to be no private ownership in any portion of that region (the Yellowstone), but the whole of it ought to be set aside as a great National Park."
—Cornelius Hedges, quoted in Langford's Diary of the
Washburn-Doane-Langford Expedition, September 20, 1870.

FOR many centuries, although a comparatively new creation geologically speaking, the Yellowstone country existed unseen, unnamed, in the heart of a continent unknown to the civilized peoples of the world. Any prehistoric occupancy of the area which may have existed certainly left no scars of use and no tradition among the Indians. Jurisdiction to the great Northwest Territory came with the Louisiana Purchase, but there existed little knowledge of the vast domain on the part of either the seller or the buyer. The Lewis and Clark Expedition, authorized by President Jefferson to explore and hold for the young Republic the great country acquired from the French, passed within fifty miles of the present Yellowstone National Park, but from the Indians at Mandan, where they spent the winter, they heard nothing of the fabulous headwaters of the Yellowstone. Whether this was due to ignorance or to reticence in mentioning what may have seemed to them manifestations of the Evil Spirit is not known. The Blackfeet, Crow, and Shoshone Indians who hunted, trapped, and fished in what we now know as Montana, Idaho, and Wyoming, probably penetrated the park on occasion, but generally avoided the region, perhaps because of its inaccessibility and its short season free from snow and bitter weather, but possibly because the boiling cauldrons and the spurting jets of steam appeared to them, like the thunder and lightning, as exhibitions of the wrath and power of the gods. The early Indian guides who entered with various exploration parties seemed unfamiliar with the terrain, but their exclamations indicated that to them the geysers and springs and paint pots were thoroughly *bad*.

The only Indians known to live in the Yellowstone country were the Sheepeaters, a tribe of small, poor, and peaceful Indians who had little property in the way of horses, clothing or permanent abodes. For food they had the mountain sheep, and they fashioned primitive utensils and weapons from obsidian.

Today the Indians no longer roam the plains. They live stodgily in the reservations which have been grudgingly granted them by the white man. They eat food from the white man's tin cans. No longer are obsidian spearpoints and utensils of any use. The Indians adopted the white man's weapons, and with firearms they have united with the white man to exterminate to a pitiful protected remnant the bison which once furnished them meat and excitement. And so we inherit the beauty of Obsidian Cliff, seen by thousands of tourists every summer in Yellowstone National Park, and no doubt worth more in revenue as an object of natural art than it ever was as an obsidian quarry.

Though Lewis and Clark missed the Yellowstone and all of its wonders, John Colter, one of their party, turned back and came into the country in 1807, probably the first white man to enter its sacred precincts. But Colter's tales seemed so "tall" to those who heard them that the country came to be known as "Colter's Hell" —a mirage in reverse action, as it were. Discredited as were his "romances" about what he had seen, he did in 1810 furnish important information for the map of the Lewis and Clark Expedition, then in course of preparation. His route of 1807, which revealed the Teton Mountains, Jackson's Hole, the source of the Snake River, the Yellowstone Lake and River, proved of much more importance to posterity than the more spectacular escape from the Indians once depicted so commonly in the geography and history books.

Except for a few trappers during the heyday of the half century which saw the exploitation of the wild fur-bearing animals in America, the Yellowstone remained uncontaminated by man. Serenely its craggy mountains lifted their peaks skyward, covered with soft blankets of snow for most of the year, their slopes strewn with bright blossoms during the short, mild summers. High on the Great Divide the headwaters of the Snake and Yellowstone trickled in little nearby rills, one toward the Gulf of Mexico and the Atlantic, the other to the Colorado and the Pacific. And nestling on the east side of the Divide were the blue waters of Lake Yellowstone, with its irregular forested shores, less than five miles from Shoshone, Lewis, and Heart Lakes, yet unnamed, on the other side of the

Divide. The brightly colored yellow stone canyon and falls, though unknown to the great American public, had an Indian name which was first translated into French and then into English, Yellow Rock or Yellow Stone. The hot springs boiled, the paint-pots bubbled, and the geysers spouted steam with none to observe. The lovely colors of the pools and the intricately fragile deposits formed and reformed, their secret beauty unseen and unheralded.

The land of enchantment seemed to hold its own protection. Its marvels were shunned by the belligerent tribes of the surrounding country; the lowly Sheepeaters seemed hardly conscious of the marvels which were near them. They left the country as they found it. The trappers caught abundant beaver and other fur-bearing animals on the plains at lower altitudes where they could set their traps in winter, when the fur was at its best. Even the gold rush to California in '49 brought no travelers into the high Yellowstone country. The wagon routes lay north or south of this seemingly impenetrable mass of mountains. In time, mining developed in Montana and other nearby States, but there was little prospecting in these snow-mantled mountains at the crest of the continent.

About the time that persistent rumors concerning the marvels of the Yellowstone might have stimulated exploration, the Civil War, which almost rent the Union in twain, came along and utilized on one side or the other all the bold spirits who might otherwise have organized expeditions into this strange country.

Although Captain Raynolds, of the Corps of Topographical Engineers, U. S. A., had, in the company of Bridger, skirted the high Yellowstone country in 1859, his report was not issued until after the close of the Civil War. In September of 1869, Messrs. Folsom, Cook and Peterson, although they failed to secure a military escort, set out to discover what actually did lie in the upper Yellowstone country. They threaded the Missouri River to Three Forks, then went by way of Bozeman and Fort Ellis to the Yellowstone, and along that river to the falls and to the lake. They crossed the mountains to Shoshone Lake and finally reached the Lower Geyser Basin. They saw the Fountain Geyser, traveled along the Firehole River to Excelsior Geyser and Prismatic Lake. Mr. Folsom wrote an account of the trip which was published in July, 1871, in the *Western Monthly* of Chicago.

The most famous and significant expedition into the Yellowstone

[3]

was the Washburn-Doane-Langford party, which made the pack-train trip in 1870. Not only did the members of this expedition see the principal features of the Yellowstone high country, but they left ample records of what they saw, and they came home with a new idea, an idea which was to create a new form of land-use in the United States.

There were nine civilian members of the party, including General Henry D. Washburn, surveyor general of Montana, who had served in the Civil War; Judge Cornelius Hedges, a distinguished member of the Montana bar; Samuel T. Hauser, a civil engineer and president of the First National Bank of Helena, afterwards Governor of Montana; Walter Trumbull, assistant assessor of internal revenue, and a son of United States Senator Lyman Trumbull of Illinois; Truman Everts, assessor of internal revenue for Montana, and Nathaniel P. Langford, who was collector of internal revenue for Montana, and who was designated as the official diarist of the trip. General Washburn was chosen captain of the party. A military escort from Fort Ellis was furnished on the order of Major General Hancock. General Chittenden, in his book published in 1895, stated that General Sheridan, who passed through Helena prior to his departure for the scene of the Franco-Prussian War, "spent some time in arranging for a military escort to accompany the party." In spite of the fact that nearly all of the men under Major Baker were in the field fighting Indians, Langford recorded that five men under the command of Lieutenant Gustavus C. Doane of the Second U. S. Cavalry were detailed, and "we are satisfied." As finally organized, there were nine civilians, six soldiers, two packers, two cooks, and thirty-five horses and mules.

Langford has given us an intensely human account of the day-by-day doings of the party, but the official report of Lieutenant Doane, which was transmitted by Secretary of War Belknap to the Committee of Territories of the United States Senate and published as Senate Document No. 51, 41st Congress, third session, contains the most complete, detailed, and penetrating descriptions to be found.

On the sixth day out, the party came to Tower Fall, where, Lieutenant Doane wrote: "A view from the summit of one of (the rock) spires is exceedingly beautiful; the clear icy stream plunges from a brink 100 feet beneath to the bottom of the chasm, over

GEYSER IN YELLOWSTONE
NATIONAL PARK

Photograph—J. E. Haynes

Courtesy—Portfolio, American Planning
and Civic Association

A WAYSIDE EXHIBIT IN YELLOW-
STONE, SHOWING HOW OBSIDIAN
CLIFF WAS FORMED

Photograph—Department of the Interior

[5]

TWO VIEWS OF OLD FAITHFUL,
YELLOWSTONE NATIONAL PARK

200 feet below, and thence rushes through the narrow gorge, tumbling over boulders and tree trunks fallen in the channel. The sides of the chasm are worn away into caverns lined with variously tinted mosses, nourished by clouds of spray which rise from the cataract; while above, and to the left, a spur from the great plateau rises above all, with a perpendicular front of 400 feet. . . . Nothing can be more chastely beautiful than this lovely cascade, hidden away in the dim light of overshadowing rocks and woods, its very voice hushed to a low murmur, unheard at the distance of a few hundred yards."

On the eighth day they came in sight of the Grand Canyon of the Yellowstone, "its perpendicular sides, wherever visible, of . . . yellow sulphuric tint . . . and its crest on either side of the river, mantled with heavy timber, extending beyond in an unbroken forest as far as the eye could reach." From here they saw their first column of steam, "rising from a dense woods to the height of several hundred feet."

At this point Lieutenant Doane confessed surprise and amazement. "We had all heard fabulous stories of this region, and were somewhat skeptical of appearances." After the trip was over Cornelius Hedges remarked, "I think a more confirmed set of skeptics never went out into the wilderness than those who composed our party, and never was a party more completely surprised and captivated with the wonders of nature."

But in the next few days of exploration when they saw so many remarkable sights, they were awed by the Falls and the Canyon of the Yellowstone as a superb spectacle. Said Lieutenant Doane: "Both of these cataracts (Upper and Lower Falls) deserve to be ranked among the great waterfalls of the continent. . . . Every cascade has a language and an idea peculiarly its own, embodied, as it were, in the flow of the waters. Thus the impression on the mind conveyed by Niagara may be summed up as 'Overwhelming power'; of the Yosemite, as 'Altitude'; of the Shoshone Fall, in the midst of the desert, as 'Going to waste.' (Alas! No longer going to waste since the power development displaced its beauty.) So the upper fall of the Yellowstone may be said to embody the idea of 'Momentum,' and the lower fall 'Gravitation.' In scenic beauty, the upper cataract fall excels the lower. It has life, animation, while the lower one simply follows its channel; both, however, are eclipsed, as it were, by the singular wonders of the mighty canyon below. This deepens rapidly; the stream flowing over rapids continually."

The ground on the brink rises also to the foot of Mt. Washburn, an eminence named for General Washburn, as, according to Cornelius Hedges, "he was the first to climb its bare, bald summit, and thence reported to us the welcome news that he saw the beautiful lake that had been the proposed object of our journey."

From then on, the expedition saw and perforce had to believe the unbelievable. Day after day, the climax of the marvels seen the day before reached new heights of beauty and of incomprehensibility. They were all practical men, living under practical frontier conditions. They had to accept the evidences of their senses. Fortunately, too, more than one of the number proved to be apperceptive to natural beauty and to possess the soul of a poet.

Curiously enough, even from these distinguished gentlemen of undoubted standing, the facts seemed too fabulous for the American public to accept. Dr. Holland, the editor of *Scribner's* (later *Century*) *Magazine*, sent to Mr. Langford a number of uncomplimentary criticisms of his articles in the May and June issues of 1871.

One reviewer said: "This Langford must be the champion liar of the Northwest." Langford confessed to a feeling of satisfaction when a letter was published later in the summer, written by a member of the U. S. Geological Survey, containing the words: "Langford did not dare tell one-half of what he saw."

Langford paid his respects to the falls and the canyon. The stupendous scene had on him a profound emotional effect. He wrote in his Diary: "The scenery surrounding the canyon and falls on both banks of the Yellowstone is enlivened by all the hues of abundant vegetation. The foothills approach the river, crowned with a vesture of evergreen pines. Meadows verdant with grasses and shrubbery stretch away to the base of the distant mountains, which, rolling into ridges, rising into peaks, and breaking into chains, are defined in the deepest blue upon the horizon. To render the scene still more imposing, remarkable volcanic deposits, wonderful boiling springs, jets of heated vapor, large collections of sulphur, immense rocks and petrifications abound in great profusion in this immediate vicinity. The river is filled with trout, and bear, elk, deer, mountain lions and lesser game roam the plains, forests and mountain fastnesses.

"The two grand falls of the Yellowstone form a fitting completion to this stupendous climax of wonders. They impart life, power, light and majesty to an assemblage of elements, which without them would be the most gloomy and horrible solitude in nature. Their eternal anthem, echoing from canyon, mountain, rock and woodland, thrills you with delight, and you gaze with rapture at the iris-crowned curtains of fleecy foam as they plunge into gulfs enveloped in mist and spray. The stillness which held your senses spellbound, as you peered into the dismal depths of the canyon below, is now broken by the uproar of waters; the terror it inspired is superseded by admiration and astonishment, and the scene, late so painful from its silence and gloom, is now animate with joy and revelry."

The descriptions of the springs, geysers and other marvels were given in great detail. Lieutenant Doane presented workmanlike word pictures of all that they saw. Langford must have written late each night after the day's explorations. According to Langford's entry on September 1: "Six miles above the upper fall we entered upon a region remarkable for the number and variety of its hot springs and craters. The principal spring, and the one that first meets the eye as you approach from the north, is a hot sulphur spring, of oval shape, the water of which is constantly boiling and is thrown up to a height of from three to seven feet. . . . Farther along the base of this mountain is a sulphurous cavern about twenty feet deep, and seven or eight feet in diameter at its mouth, out of which the steam is thrown in jets with a sound resembling the puffing of a steamboat when laboring over a sandbar, and with as much uniformity and intonation as if emitted by a high-pressure engine. From hundreds of fissures in the adjoining mountain from base to summit, issue hot sulphur vapors, the apertures through which they escape being encased in thick incrustations of sulphur. . . . . There are nearby a number of small sulphur springs. . . . .

"About one hundred yards from these springs is a large hot spring of irregular shape, but averaging forty feet long by twenty-five wide, the water of which is a dark muddy color. Still farther on are twenty or thirty springs of boiling mud of different degrees of consistency and color. . . . The mud in these springs is in most

[9]

cases a little thinner than mortar prepared for plastering, and, as it is thrown up from one to two feet, I can liken its appearance to nothing so much as Indian meal hasty pudding when the process of boiling is nearly completed, except that the puffing, bloated bubbles are greatly magnified, being from a few inches to two feet in diameter. In some of the springs the mud is of a dark brown color, in others nearly pink, and in one it was almost yellow. . . .

"All of these springs are embraced within a circle the radius of which is from a thousand to twelve hundred feet, and the whole of this surface seems to be a smothered crater covered over with an incrustation of sufficient strength and thickness to bear usually a very heavy weight, but which in several instances yielded and even broke through under the weight of our horses as we rode over it. . . . Under the whole of this incrustation the hottest fire seemed to be raging, and the heat issuing from the vents or from the crevices caused from the breaking in of the surface is too intense to be borne by the gloved hand for an instant."

Even in the midst of the incredible performances in the basins, Langford found words of admiration for Yellowstone Lake. Said he: "Yellowstone Lake, as seen from our camp tonight (September 3, 1870), seems to me to be the most beautiful body of water in the world. In front of our camp it has a wide sandy beach like that of the ocean, which extends for miles and as far as the eye can reach, save that occasionally there is to be found a sharp projection of rocks. The overlooking bench rises from the water's edge about eight feet, forming a bank of sand or natural levee, which serves to prevent the overflow of the land adjoining, which, when the lake is receiving the water from the mountain streams that empty into it while the snows are melting, is several feet below the surface of the lake. . . . From our camp we can see several islands from five to ten miles distant in a direct line. Two of the three 'Tetons,' which are so plainly visible to travelers going to Montana from Eagle Rock bridge on Snake River, and which are such well known and prominent landmarks on that stage route, we notice tonight."

Along the Yellowstone River the party had followed Indian and game trails for the most part, but when they struck out to follow the borders of the lake around the south side they were obliged to find their way through forests where the down timber had never been cleared—and never is a long time! On the 7th of September

[10]

Langford and Doane went on a scouting tour to determine the best line of travel to follow in passing around the lake. Langford remarked in his Diary: "There is just enough excitement attending these scouting expeditions to make them a real pleasure, overbalancing the labor attendant upon them. There is very little probability that any large band of Indians will be met with on this side of the lake, owing to the superstitions which originate in the volcanic forces here found."

He climbed a mountain where he thought "the view from the summit of this mountain, for wild and rugged grandeur, is surpassed by none I ever before saw. The Yellowstone basin and the Wind River mountains were spread out before us like a map. On the south the eye followed the source of the Yellowstone above the lake, until, twenty-five miles away, it was lost in an immense canyon, beyond which two immense jets of vapor rose to a height of probably three hundred feet, indicating that there were other and perhaps greater wonders than those embraced in our prescribed limit of exploration. On the north the outlet of the lake and the steam from the mud geyser and mud volcano were distinctly visible, while on the southeast the view followed to the horizon a succession of lofty peaks and ridges at least thirty miles in width, whose jagged slopes were filled with yawning caverns, pine-embowered recesses and beetling precipices, some hundreds and some thousands of feet in height. This is the range which Captain Raynolds, approaching from the east, found impassable while on his exploring tour to the Yellowstone in the year 1860. . . .

"The valley at the base of this range was dotted with small lakes. Lakes abound everywhere—in the valleys, on the mountains and further down on their slopes at all elevations. . . .

"This range of mountains has a marvelous history. As it is the loftiest, so it is probably the most remarkable lateral ridge of the Rocky range. In the expedition sent across the continent by Mr. Astor, in 1811, under command of Captain Wilson P. Hunt, that gentleman met with the first serious obstacle to his progress at the eastern base of this range. After numerous efforts to scale it, he turned away and followed the valley of Snake River, encountering the most discouraging disasters until he arrived at Astoria. . . . I have read somewhere . . . that the Indians regard this ridge of mountains as the crest of the world, and that among the Blackfeet there is a fable that he who attains its summit catches a view of the 'Land of Souls' and beholds the 'Happy Hunting Grounds' spread out below him, brightening with the abodes of the free and generous spirits."

The next day the party zigzagged over fallen timber—"a terrible day for both men and horses." It was while traversing this trackless forest, with the attendant difficulties of urging on the pack train and extricating the horses when wedged between trees, requiring re-adjustment of the packs, that Mr. Everts became separated from the party for thirty-seven days of peril until he was rescued by a scouting party some time after the return of the expedition. After vain searching and delay until provisions began to run short, the expedition pushed on around the thumb of the lake to the Upper and Lower Geyser Basins on the Firehole River. They came upon and named Old Faithful, then, as now, erupting steam and hot water at regular intervals. In announcing the start on the 16th of September for the search of the Firehole basin, Mr. Langford remarked: "Our journey around Yellowstone Lake in close proximity to the beach is doubtless the first ever attempted; and, although it has been attended with difficulty and distress, these have been to me as nothing compared with the enjoyment the journey has afforded, and it is with the greatest regret that I turn my face from it home-wards."

But the form of the future was not yet quite cast. Langford re-marked on the evening of the 16th in his Diary, concerning the lake: "It is dotted with islands of great beauty, as yet unvisited by man, but which at no remote period will be adorned with villas and the ornaments of civilized life. The winds from the mountain gorges roll its placid waters into a furious sea, and crest its billows with foam. Forests of pine, deep, dark and almost impenetrable, are scattered at random along its banks, and its beautiful margin pre-sents every variety of sand and pebbly beach, glittering with crystals, carnelians and chalcedony. . . . . It possesses adaptabilities for the highest display of artificial culture, amid the greatest wonders of Nature that the world affords, and is beautified by the grandeur of the most extensive mountain scenery, and not many years can elapse before the march of civil improvement will reclaim this delightful solitude, and garnish it with all the attractions of cultivated taste and refinement."

Twice they crossed the main divide and encountered snow, and what with the loss of one of their number, short rations and the accumulated fatigue of the journey, the members of the expedition were low in their minds. Imagine their revivification when they came upon Old Faithful and the many other geysers and springs which they named. Many of these names survive to the present day. Langford commented: "The water in some of the springs presents to the eye the colors of all the precious gems known to commerce. In one spring the hue is like that of an emerald, in another like that of a turquoise, another has the ultramarine hue of the sapphire, another has the color of the topaz; and the suggestion has been made that the names of these jewels may very properly be given to many of these springs."

But now the form of the future was to be cast. On Tuesday, September 20, Langford recorded in his Diary: "Last night, and also this morning in camp, the entire party had a rather unusual discussion. The proposition was made by some member that we utilize the result of our exploration by taking up quarter sections of land at the most prominent points of interest, and a general discussion followed. One member of our party suggested that if there could be secured by pre-emption a good title to two or three quarter sections of land opposite the lower fall of the Yellowstone and extending down the river along the canyon, they would eventually become a source of great profit to the owners. Another member of the party thought that it would be more desirable to take up a quarter section of land at the Upper Geyser Basin, for the reason that that locality could be more easily reached by tourists and pleasure seekers. A third suggestion was that each member of the party pre-empt a claim, and in order that no one should have an advantage over the others, the whole should be thrown into a common pool for the benefit of the entire party.

"Mr. Hedges then said that he did not approve of any of these plans—that there ought to be no private ownership of any portion of that region, but that the whole of it ought to be set apart as a great National Park, and that each one of us ought to make an effort to have this accomplished. His suggestion met with an instantaneous and favorable response from all—except one—of the members of our party, and each hour since the matter was first broached, our enthusiasm has increased. It has been the main theme of our conversation today as we journeyed. I lay awake half of last night thinking about it;—and if my wakefulness deprived my bedfellow (Hedges) of any sleep, he has only himself and his disturbing national-park proposition to answer for it.

"Our purpose to create a park can only be accomplished by untiring work and concerted action in a warfare against the incredulity and unbelief of our national legislators when our proposal shall be presented for their approval. Nevertheless, I believe we can win the battle.

"I do not know of any portion of our country where a national park can be established furnishing to visitors more wonderful attractions than here. These wonders are so different from anything we have ever seen—they are so various, so extensive—that the feeling in my mind from the moment they began to appear until we left them has been one of intense surprise and of incredulity. Every day spent in surveying them has revealed to me some new beauty, and now that I have left them, I begin to feel a skepticism which clothes them in a memory clouded by doubt."

Langford closed his Diary with an entry on September 27 at Helena, Montana: "My narrations have excited great wonder, and I cannot resist the conviction that many of my auditors believe that I have 'drawn a long bow' in my descriptions. I am perfectly free to acknowledge that this does not surprise me. It seems a most natural thing for them to do so; for, in the midst of my narrations, I find myself almost as ready to doubt the reality of the scenes I have attempted to describe as the most skeptical of my listeners. They pass along my memory like the faintly defined outlines of a dream. And when I dwell upon their strange peculiarities, their vastness, their variety, and the distinctive features of novelty which mark them all, so entirely out of the range of all objects that compose the natural scenery and wonders of this continent, I who have seen them can scarcely realize that in those far-off recesses of the mountains they have existed so long in impenetrable seclusion, and that hereafter they will stand foremost among the natural attractions of the world. Astonishment and wonder become so firmly impressed upon the mind in the presence of these objects, that belief stands appalled, and incredulity is dumb. You can see Niagara, comprehend its beauties, and carry from it a memory ever ready to summon before you all its grandeur. You can stand in the valley of the

[14]

Yosemite, and look up its mile of vertical granite, and distinctly recall its minutest feature; but amid the canyon and falls, the boiling springs and sulphur mountain, and, above all, the mud volcano and and the geysers of the Yellowstone, your memory becomes filled and clogged with objects new in experience, wonderful in extent, and possessing unlimited grandeur and beauty. It is a new phase in the natural world; a fresh exhibition of the handiwork of the Great Architect; and, while you see and wonder, you seem to need an additional sense, fully to comprehend and believe."

The Washburn-Doane-Langford expedition laid before the reading world a description of a little known and seldom explored region, as it penetrated, probably, beyond any former explorations. But its historical significance lies in the birth of a new idea—an idea closely connected with democracy—the idea of the common ownership of land and resources, dedicated to the use and enjoyment of the people. This idea is the more remarkable that it overlaps the era of individual enterprise on the part of the American people—an era in which the Federal Government was still making persistent efforts to push public lands into private ownership. The idea, too, of recognizing enjoyment as of importance was novel, for the people of the United States were, for the most part, still strongly in thrall to the Puritan objective of hard work. It was distinctly a new thing to recognize communion with Nature as desirable.

Since the expedition of 1870, many scientific parties have conducted research in the Yellowstone and have published their findings. There were the famous expeditions under Hayden, Powell, King, and Wheeler. There was the expedition of the Engineer Corps of the Army, with Captains Barlow and Heap in charge. This expedition was accompanied by Thomas Moran, whose pictures made the Yellowstone famous, and by W. H. Jackson, who brought back many authentic photographs. Jackson at 96 is still hale and hearty, and visits the Yellowstone and Tetons annually. Dr. Hayden visited the region again in 1872 and again in 1878, which resulted in the publication in 1883 of a comprehensive report by Dr. Hayden and his associates.

In an introduction, written to precede a reprint of his Diary in 1905, Mr. Langford stated that the question has frequently been asked him, "Who originated the plan of setting apart this region as a National Park?" Mr. Langford's statement follows: "I answer

[15]

that Judge Cornelius Hedges of Helena wrote the first articles ever published by the press urging the dedication of this region as a park. The *Helena Herald* of November 9, 1870, contains a letter of Mr. Hedges, in which he advocated the scheme, and in my lectures delivered in Washington and New York in January of 1871, I directed attention to Mr. Hedges' suggestion and urged the passage by Congress of an act setting apart that region as a public park. All this was several months prior to the first exploration by the U. S. Geological Survey, in charge of Dr. Hayden. The suggestion that the region should be made into a National Park was first broached to the members of our party on September 19, 1870, by Mr. Hedges, while we were in camp at the confluence of the Firehole and Gibbon Rivers, as related in this Diary. After the return home of our party, I was informed by General Washburn that on the eve of the departure of our expedition from Helena, David E. Folsom had suggested to him the desirability of creating a park at the grand canyon and falls of the Yellowstone. This fact was unknown to Mr. Hedges— and the boundary lines of the proposed park were extended by him so as to be commensurate with the wider range of our explorations."

The evidence would indicate that Cornelius Hedges was the first to make known the concept of a great national park for all the people. Probably, as in the case of many inventions, the idea may have been in the air and caught up by different persons, almost simultaneously. Whether Dr. Hayden heard of the project from some of the Washburn expedition or whether some such idea was forming in his own mind, we may never know.

Once the idea was conceived, the next step was to bring about its realization. There were two great obstacles to this. Legislative bodies are prone to be conservative. They hesitate to try new plans, except in time of revolution when educational campaigns have assumed an emotional appeal. The idea of a national park provided by the Federal Government was new indeed; but the description of the region, however faithful, could hardly be expected to carry conviction to a Congress composed then, as now, of many town lawyers and few who had participated in pioneering explorations.

Every bit of help which could be mustered was needed. Langford went to Washington in the winter of 1871–72. He delivered lectures there and in New York. Before he left Montana for the East, he, Cornelius Hedges, and the newly elected delegate to Congress from the Territory of Montana adopted a tentative plan of action. Langford and Delegate Clagett apparently drew the act of dedication, except for the boundary descriptions which they secured from Dr. Hayden. Mr. Clagett introduced the bill into the House on December 18, 1871. Senator Pomeroy introduced it into the Senate. As is usual, after the bill was referred to the Committee on Public Lands in each house, the chairman of the sub-committee in the House having the bill in charge, addressed a letter to the Secretary of the Interior, who, on January 29, 1872, endorsed the measure. With the letter came a brief report by Dr. Hayden, who was in a strategic position. A scientist of note who had, on behalf of the Federal Government, visited the area in person, secured convincing scientific data, specimens, and numerous photographs, could hardly be disbelieved. Dr. Hayden was enthusiastic. He and Langford visited personally practically every member of Congress. Four hundred copies of Langford's articles in the May and June *Scribner's Magazine* were placed on the desks of members of Congress at the psychological date when the bill was to be voted on. The result was that the Senate passed the bill on January 30, the House on February 27, and on March 1, 1872, President Grant signed the bill.

The wording of the act is little short of a masterpiece. The described area is by the act "reserved and withdrawn from settlement, occupancy or sale under the laws of the United States, and dedicated and set apart as a public park or pleasuring ground for the benefit and enjoyment of the people." The park was to be under the exclusive control of the Secretary of the Interior, who was directed to make regulations which "shall provide for the preservation from injury or spoliation of all timber, mineral deposits, natural curiosities or wonders within said park, and their retention in their natural condition." Thus was a policy declared at the outset—a policy of conservation applied to a new kind of area. The act included guidance for the sort of administration which should be set up and for the sort of facilities which it was thought would be required. The Secretary was authorized, in his discretion, to "grant leases for building purposes, for terms not exceeding ten years, of small parcels of ground, at such places in said park as shall require the erection of buildings for the accommodation of visitors," and "all of the proceeds of said leases, and all other revenues that may be derived from any source connected with the park" were "to be expended under his direction in the management of the same, and the construction of roads and bridle-paths," and "shall provide against the wanton destruction of the fish and game found within the park, and against their capture or destruction for the purposes of merchandise or profit." Though it has been necessary to amend the act in order to develop a responsible administration and settle many troublesome problems, today the original act is still the guiding star for the administration of Yellowstone National Park.

Neither Delegate Clagett nor Mr. Langford seems to have known of it, but it transpired that Dr. Hayden, in order to muster votes for the bill, must have made promises that Congress would not be called on for some time for funds for the park. Such promises are not unknown, even in recent legislation! At any rate, no money was forthcoming from Congress. Mr. Langford served as superintendent of the park for five years without pay and with no money for protection or development. His assistant superintendents also served without pay. In the 1905 introduction to his Diary, Mr. Langford stated that in the second year of his services as superintendent, some of his friends in Congress proposed to give him a salary sufficiently large to pay actual expenses. But, he declared, "I requested them to make no effort in this behalf, saying that I feared that some successful applicant for such a salaried position, giving little thought to the matter, would approve the applications for leases; and that as long as I could prevent the granting of any exclusive concessions I would be willing to serve as superintendent without compensation." It was, perhaps, during this period that Langford's friends suggested that his initials N. P. stood for "National Park," and he sometimes wrote in the Spencerian script of the day, "National Park" Langford.

As soon as the park was created, applications began to pour in on the Secretary of the Interior for leases and concessions of all sorts. Apparently, many people thought that they could still "take up" land within the park. As soon as the region became known, all sorts of merchants, ranchers, and inn-keepers from far and near applied for licenses to operate concessions. It mattered not that many of them knew nothing of mountain or pioneer conditions.

Hunters also gave much trouble. Even today it is most difficult to withdraw areas from hunting. Hunters seem to believe that they have a vested right to stalk game on publicly owned lands. In the interests of conservation and in the face of the rapid disappearance of game, the States now enforce rigorous laws for open and closed seasons and for licensing hunters and fishermen. Today Yellowstone and all other national parks are game sanctuaries. Commercial fishing is barred and no hunting is allowed, but visitors to the national parks may enjoy the age-old Waltonian fishing pastime under ideally protected conditions. In the seventies, however, the wagon roads which opened up the park brought in many hunters from the vicinity. It was physically impossible to protect an area of over 3,000 square miles of the most rugged character in the country. Were it not for the protection given wildlife in national parks and established refuges, there would be no hunting anywhere!

Mr. Langford, who had been fired by a fine conception and a high sense of service, was frustrated at every turn. He was criticized by the local papers. He was given no help and no funds from Washington. Uncle Sam, having good-naturedly granted, through Congress, the petition of the little band of enthusiasts, apparently had no realization that he had taken on any responsibilities. The act still read well, but the practice was disappointing. Langford's disillusionment was, at the end of five years, almost complete. It seems a miracle that the park project was not abandoned. Only in after years could Langford look back on the service which he and his friends had rendered as leading to the establishment of an enduring national park—the first of its kind in the United States.

In 1877, P. W. Norris of Michigan came into the park as superintendent. His reports to the Secretary of the Interior are most illuminating. He sought appropriations for roads. He was obliged to complain about the depredations of the American tourist. He was succeeded by incompetent and unwise superintendents, most of whom entered upon their duties with no knowledge of the country or climate, and several of whom were involved in scandals concerning concessions and private gain. In 1855, when Congress declined to appropriate money for the administration of the park, the Secretary of the Interior called upon the Secretary of War for troops to patrol the park, as he was authorized to do by an Act of Congress passed in 1883. For more than thirty years soldiers manned the park.

General Hiram M. Chittenden, who served in his early military days as Assistant Officer in charge for the two years, 1891–2, published a book on "The Yellowstone National Park" in 1895. Beginning in 1899, General Chittenden began a second tour of duty in the park, in charge of road-building. His name, therefore, is closely associated with all that is best in the park. His book, which has gone through many editions, remains one of the standard works on Yellowstone. He was responsible for valuable research, was sympathetic with park aims, and believed in preserving the park as nearly as possible in its natural condition.

In 1918, the year after the National Park Service was created, the War Department was relieved of its responsibilities in the park, and on June 28, 1919, Horace M. Albright became superintendent of Yellowstone National Park. During the ten years that Mr. Albright served as superintendent, a new system of administration was developed, the services of park rangers perfected, and the principles of park protection crystallized. A number of serious assaults on the integrity of the park were launched by politicians during this period, but, with the aid of public opinion and conservation organizations, the National Park Service was enabled to withstand all raids on the Yellowstone. When Mr. Albright became Director of the National Park Service early in 1929, he was succeeded by Roger Toll, of Colorado, who served until his tragic death in 1936. He was succeeded by Edmund Rogers, also of Colorado, who is now in charge of the park.

In spite of early difficulties and discouragements, in spite of initial mistakes and neglects, Yellowstone is now firmly established as an outstanding national park in a system of national parks which are created and administered along lines set forth in the act of dedication in 1872. A new and special form of land-use has been inaugurated which meets with favor in the eyes of the American people. They are both landlords and tenants in common of lands administered for their benefit and enjoyment. It was this phrase from the act of dedication that was carved into the entrance gate at Gardiner, where, on April 24, 1903, President Theodore Roosevelt laid the corner-stone:

For the benefit and enjoyment of the people.

  Courtesy—Portfolio, American Planning and Civic Association

HALF DOME, AT THE HEAD OF YOSEMITE VALLEY

[21]

TEN-EI-YA AND YOSEMITE

"I will not leave my home, but be with the spirits among the rocks, the water-falls, in the rivers and in the winds; wheresoever you go I will be with you. You will not see me, but you will fear the spirit of the old chief, and grow cold. The great spirits have spoken!"

—Quoted from Chief Ten-ei-ya by Dr. L. H. Bunnell
in "Discovery of the Yosemite," 1880.

WHEN Yosemite Valley became known to the white settlers of California, some twenty years before the famous Washburn expedition advertised Yellowstone to the American public, it was the well-beloved home of a band of Indians closely related to the Monos whose hunting-grounds were on the east side of the Sierra Nevada Mountains. Curiously inaccessible, in the heart of the high Sierra peaks, snow-bound in the winter months, the valley was unknown to the *padres* and Spanish *dons*. A small band of warlike Indians—Yosemites by name—occupied the valley as their stronghold. They built encampments—*rancheries*, as the Spanish called them—and stored acorns on the floor of the valley. Their trails led to natural caverns and recesses in the granite rocks, to which they could retire in case of attack.

Within Indian memory or tradition no white man had ever entered or seen the valley before 1851, though some of the early American settlers had heard of the "deep valley" of the Yosemites from their Indian friends. Few Indians unrelated to the Yosemites had ever been allowed to penetrate into the valley. In winter the trails over the crests to the land of the Monos were impassable. The lofty granite walls and high peaks and ridges gave the home of the Yosemites a protection which few man-built fortresses could command.

For centuries after the Great Artist, using colossal glaciers for etching tools, had carved the magic picture, the valley may have existed alone, unseen and unknown even to the Indians. In the 1850's, the Yosemites, numbering about two hundred, lived in this enchanted valley. When the American settlers came into the Mariposa country, south of the valley, the Yosemites resented and feared them. The old chief sent out raiding parties to murder and rob the settlers and burn their settlements. It was a military expedition in 1851, to bring the defiant Yosemites into proposed peace pacts with the United States Government—the Great White Father—that introduced the first white men into the enchanted valley.

[23]

The scant contact with the Sierra Nevada Mountains before 1851 may be told in a few words. California was in communication with the eastern seaboard by boat via Cape Horn before the hardy pioneers crossed the high crests of the stubborn Sierra. To Jedediah Smith, a fur trader, is given the credit for the first transcontinental journey to California. In 1826 he led an exploring party from the Great Salt Lake. In California he was met with the opposition of the Spanish Governor, who saw no good to his domain from the exploiting trade of the American trappers. After long and laborious mountain travel into regions unpenetrated by the Spanish, Smith and his followers worked their way from the region of the Cajon Pass to the San Joaquin Valley. They saw "few beaver and elk, deer and antelope in abundance," and so they started back to the Great Salt Lake across the Sierra Nevada, where the peaks pierce the clouds and the valleys are deep between steep granite walls. They found the route, probably north of Yosemite Valley, beset with hardships and difficulties, but lived to return another day.

A good many fur trappers and traders, in the next few years, traveled into California over the mountains. They brought back fabulous and alluring stories of the pleasant land of sunshine which lay beyond the snow-capped granite guardian walls. One division of Captain Bonneville's exploring party, under Joseph Walker, reached California through the Humboldt Valley, south of Carson Lake. They probably threaded the ridge between the Tuolumne and Merced Rivers into the high Yosemite country, but the Indian guides later reported that they purposely led the explorers by a route which would avoid the valley.

Washington Irving, in 1837, wrote an account of Bonneville's expedition, and Zeno Leonard, who accompanied the Walker party, published in 1839 a narrative of the trip. They must have seen some of the finest views in the high Sierra. According to the Leonard account: "We traveled for miles every day, still on top of the mountains, and our course continually obstructed with snow hills and rocks. Here we began to encounter in our path many small streams which would shoot out from under these high snow-banks, and after running a short distance in deep chasms which they have through the ages cut in the rocks, precipitate themselves from one lofty precipice to another, until they are exhausted in rain below. Some of these precipices appeared to us to be more than a mile high."

Also Leonard mentioned "some trees of the redwood species, in-credibly large—some of which would measure from 16 to 18 fathoms round the trunk at the height of a man's head from the ground."

Other curious travelers penetrated the region. Then came the settlers—that motley procession of the adventurous, the dissatisfied and the optimistic. They came into the promised land on foot, on horseback and later in wagons, following to their sources the rivers from the Gila to the Truckee.

The Spanish did not welcome the Americans. They were con-temptuous of American money-grubbing enterprise. And the easy-going, luxury-loving Spanish-Californians feared the self-sacrific-ing, energetic pioneers of the wilderness. Dr. Carl Russell, in his book, "100 Years in Yosemite," quoted the Mexican, Castro, as having stated before the Assembly in Monterey: "Those Ameri-cans are so contriving that some day they will build ladders to touch the sky, and once in the heavens they will change the whole face of the Universe and even the color of the stars."

In 1848 the "contriving" Americans had taken over California, for better or for worse, and the process of change soon began, for the discovery of gold a few months after California became a part of the United States brought the "forty-niners," the greatest army of "diggers" ever assembled. If gold could have been secured at the cost of destroying the fair surface of the entire range of colorful mountains, no doubt the Sierra Nevada today would be desecrated by deserts of desolate piles and pits of waste and slag. Fortunately, the scars of picks and shovels in the hands of pigmy prospectors could do little damage to the gigantic Sierra. And the big, ma-chine-worked mines were, in comparison to the size and extent of the mountain range, few and far between. But the height of the gold rush was over before that momentous day on which white men first saw the incomparable Yosemite Valley. The Sierra barrier between the East and the West had been conquered, though the flinty-hearted cliffs and the marauding Indians claimed tolls in death and disaster, and hardship was exacted from all who crossed these mighty mountains.

It was not until 1851, after the Sierra slopes had become infested with prospectors and some sizable mines put into operation, that the Americans actually saw the Yosemite Valley. James Savage, who probably had participated in at least one of Fremont's famous expeditions, had established in 1849–50 a trading post not more than fifteen miles below the Yosemite Valley. He knew and understood the Indians. He was adopted into many of the friendly foothill tribes. It is recorded that the five wives he took from different tribes gave him direct access to Indian gossip. The Indians had confidence in him. The squaws dug gold for him. Indeed the Indians brought gold dust into his trading post in exchange for trinkets of little value in American markets, though it must be remembered that gold had no value in inter-Indian markets. Savage was a born leader, generally esteemed by the settlers and revered by the Indians, though his profits at his trading posts were a bit on the profiteering side, unless the risk of doing business at all be taken into due consideration.

And all during these years of settlement, in a supposedly impregnable stronghold in the high Sierra, was this band of warlike Yosemites who stole horses and stock from the settlers and raided their posts with fire and pillage. Late in 1850, raids on Savage's Fresno and Mariposa stores resulted in the death of those in charge, and aroused an indignant resistance which led to an Indian war. Many of the hitherto friendly Indians were induced to join in the war against "the white gold diggers," to drive the white men from their mountains. The Indians were told by the belligerent chiefs that the white men would run from them, and that those who joined in the war would be the first to secure the property of the gold diggers. Particularly, they coveted horses, live-stock, clothing.

After other raids and cruel murders, a punitive party of settlers marched "among the densely wooded mountains in pursuit of the savages," but the Indians were able to repulse the settlers, and escape. The hastily brought together defense company had few supplies, lacked organization and collective training. Savage had joined the expedition, which, with about 100 men, tried to capture some 500 fighting Indians from the Yosemite, Chow-chilla, Kah-we-ah and other tribes. In a surprise attack by the settlers, an instigating Indian chief was killed, and the Indians retired to the mountains.

The Indian war was on. The famous Mariposa Battalion was organized, under a proclamation by Governor McDougal calling for volunteers to prevent further outrages and to punish the marauders. On January 24, 1851, the volunteers were mustered into the service. They provided their own horses and equipment. The

State furnished camp supplies and baggage trains, and the Federal Government paid the expense of maintenance, but the battalion was under the direction of the Indian Commissioners. Savage was chosen leader and commissioned as Major. While the battalion was waiting for the Commissioners to act, the depredations of the Indians continued. Part of the battalion was assigned to the Kings and Kah-we-ah Rivers and part to the San Joaquin and Merced. These volunteer soldiers went out to wage a strange war. Their instructions were to capture the Indians in their strongholds and escort them safely into the Commissioners' camp on the Fresno.

With the northern party rode a young doctor, L. H. Bunnell by name, who had come to California from New York by way of Detroit and western wilds, and who had learned something of Indian languages and psychology. Thirty years after, he wrote an excellent and interesting account of the first brief foray and the later sojourn in the Yosemite Valley in 1851.

Major Savage with his men rode toward the "deep valley" over the Black Ridge to the South Fork of the Merced. They encountered deep, damp snow which impeded their progress. But finally they surprised a Noot-chu village on the banks of the Merced. They persuaded Chief Pon-wat-chee to send his people in to the Commissioners and to aid the soldiers in bringing in the Yosemites.

Ten-ei-ya, the old chief of the Yosemites, was induced to come to the battalion camp. Major Savage, according to Dr. Bunnell, told the chief that "if he would go to the Commissioners and make a treaty of peace with them, as the other Indians were going to do, there would be no more war." But Dr. Bunnell has reported that Ten-ei-ya declared with dignity: "My people do not want anything from the 'Great Father' you tell me about. The Great Spirit is our father, and he has always supplied us with all we need. We do not want anything from white men. Our women are able to do our work. Go, then; let us remain in the mountains where we were born; where the ashes of our fathers have been given to the winds. . . . My people do not want to go to the plains."

Major Savage gave the old chief an ultimatum. "Your people must go to the Commissioners and make terms with them. If they do not, your young men will again steal our horses, your people will again kill and plunder the whites. It was your people who robbed my stores, burned my houses, and murdered my men. If they do not make a treaty, your whole tribe will be destroyed. Not one of them will be left alive." Sadly Chief Ten-ei-ya promised to send runners to bring his people in. But they did not come, and so it was decided to go to the village of the Yosemites.

Leaving a camp guard, Major Savage and his men, accompanied by Ten-ei-ya, proceeded over the ridge between the South Fork and the main Merced River. After they crossed the divide they encountered deep snow. Before they reached the valley they met seventy-two Yosemites coming in, all, explained Ten-ei-ya, who were willing to go to the plains. In the belief that the others were in hiding, as it was impossible at this time of year even for Indians to cross the high snow-enshrouded pass to reach the friendly Mono Indians on the east side of the mountains, Major Savage decided to go to the Indian village in the "deep valley."

It was as the party traveled that they suddenly came in full view of the valley of the Yosemites. Dr. Bunnell, who had once caught a glimpse of the "stupendous rocky peaks of the Sierra Nevada" while ascending the old Bear Valley trail from Ridley's ferry, on the Merced River, realized that what he had almost thought a dream was indeed a reality. "The face of the immense cliff," as the marching company saw it, "was shadowed by the declining sun." These were the first white men to behold El Capitan from the place we now call Inspiration Point.

Young Dr. Bunnell was greatly moved. "The grandeur of the scene was but softened by the haze that hung over the valley— light as gossamer—and by the clouds which partially dimmed the higher cliffs and mountains. This obscurity of vision but increased the awe with which I beheld it, and as I looked, a peculiar exalted sensation seemed to fill my whole being, and I found my eyes in tears with emotion." Dr. Bunnell had left the trail and his horse and wallowed alone to a projecting rock to examine the view. But he found scant sympathy from Major Savage or the other intrepid volunteers who were there on business bent—bringing in the Indians who were stealing their property and threatening lives.

That night the party camped on the floor of the valley around blazing fires, a memorable occasion and forerunner of many a later-day campfire. But these were soldiers—pro tem. at least—and there was no Hedges to think of "saving the valley for others." As a matter of hard fact, it is probable that most of those hardy pioneers on that March winter night could not conceive that *anybody* would be in the least bit interested in a place so hard to reach and so gloomy in the early lengthening shadows. Indeed, young Dr. Bunnell remarked that it might appear sentimental, but that "the coarse jokes of the careless, and the indifference of the practical, sensibly jarred my more devout feelings . . . as if a sacred subject had been ruthlessly profaned, or the visible power of Deity disregarded." The campers did take seriously, however, the suggestion made by Dr. Bunnell that the valley should have a name, and they voted to adopt the name "Yosemity," the name of the Indians they had come to capture. Major Savage explained to them that the name "Yo-sem-i-ty" as pronounced by Ten-ei-ya, or "O-soom-i-ty" as pronounced by some other bands, signified a full-grown grizzly bear—given to Ten-ei-ya's band "because of their lawless and predatory character." Dr. Bunnell explained in his book that it was not until 1852 that Lieutenant Moore, of the U. S. Army, in his report first adopted the spelling "Yosemite," without, however, changing the pronunciation.

Ten-ei-ya, who was present at this first campfire of those who came to invade the homes of his people, explained that he was the descendant of an Ah-wah-ne-chee chief, and that the valley was called Ah-wah-nee. But Yosemite it is today and has been ever since that March campfire in 1851. Thus was the Yosemite discovered and named.

Ten-ei-ya gave assurance that no white man had ever before visited the valley. One reason he had consented to go to the Commissioners' camp and make peace was that he hoped to prevent an expedition into the valley and that he and his people might be allowed to return to their homes. He explained that the entrance to the valley had always been carefully guarded. The valley was theirs and they had put a spell on it that, they thought, would hold it sacred for themselves alone. No other Indians, declared Ten-ei-ya, ventured to enter the valley, except by his permission; "all feared the witches" and his displeasure. He had "made war upon the white gold diggers to drive them from the mountains, and prevent their entrance into Ah-wah-nee."

After that first soldiers' campfire, the party next day crossed the Merced by ford, and marched toward El Capitan. They found recently deserted Indian huts near its base. Later, near the Royal Arches, then unnamed, they found an encampment, and another near the base of Half Dome, also deserted. Finally, the search for the Yosemites hidden in the rocky fastnesses was abandoned.

The men were more concerned with their mission than with the aspect of the valley they had discovered. As Dr. Bunnell remarked, anent the solemn grandeur of the valley and the hardships of travel which involved the frequent crossing of torrential streams of cold water: "We were not a party of tourists seeking recreation, nor philosophers investigating the operations of nature. Our business there was to find Indians who were endeavoring to escape our *charitable* intentions toward them. But very few of the volunteers seemed to have any appreciation of the wonderful proportions of the enclosing granite rocks; their curiosity had been to see the stronghold of the enemy, and the general verdict was that it was gloomy enough."

Dr. Bunnell described to Major Savage the "side trips" he had made around Mirror Lake, and the views from the cliff up North Canyon and the fall of the South Canyon. He remarked: "Yosemite must be beautifully grand a few weeks later when the foliage and flowers are at their prime, and the rush of waters has somewhat subsided. Such cliffs and water-falls I never saw before, and I doubt if they exist in any other place."

But the Major declared: "The annoyances and disappointments of a fruitless search, together with the certainty of a snow storm approaching, makes all this beautiful scenery appear to me gloomy enough. In a word, it is what we supposed it to be before seeing it, a hell of a place."

The benevolence of the battalion was not appreciated by the Yosemites and they escaped before they reached the Commissioners' camp. Major Savage started out at the head of a second "round-up" expedition, but was recalled by the Commissioners, and the command proceeded under Captain Boling. Again young Dr. Bunnell accompanied the party, at times serving as interpreter and occasionally as surgeon. The volunteer soldiers went after the Chow-chillas, who had induced the Yosemites to slip away. Their route led them into the Upper San Joaquin. They burned the lodges and acorn stores of a deserted village where the embers of a funeral pyre still glowed. The Indians themselves retired before the raiding party, offering to fight only when they had the advantage. The destruction of their lodges and stores seemed to Captain Boling the only way to force them to come in to the Commissioners. Left alone in the mountains, they were sure to continue to murder the settlers. The men in the battalion, under severe provocation and in face of shouted taunts from little bands of Indians safely sheltered in rocky coves, did quite consistently refrain from shooting Indians on sight. Even when the Indians rolled down huge stones from above in order to annihilate the pursuing men, they contented themselves with trying to preserve their own safety, and followed, so far as they could, the orders of the Commissioners. If it had not been for the responsible leadership in the battalion, the story might have been a far less creditable one.

Following the return of the battalion to the Commissioners' camp, Major Savage met with the Chow-chillas and Kah-we-ahs at a feast provided by him, and treaties of peace were signed. Dr. Bunnell reported that the Chow-chillas, who had often joined with the Yosemites in raiding parties and in the Indian war, became the most tractable of the mountain Indians. This left the Yosemites as the only important mountain tribe still at war with the settlers. Chief Ten-ei-ya had resisted all the bribes and blandishments of the Commissioners. He and his braves wanted the freedom of their mountain home.

A division of the battalion, under Captain Boling, therefore, went after the Yosemites. During this second stay in the valley the soldiers played a catch-as-catch-can game with scattered parties of Indians occupying the high places, always ready and willing to roll stones down on the adventurous who scrambled too far up the rocky trails. Finally, from a perch on a high ledge above Mirror Lake, where his retreat had been cut off from above, the old Chief Ten-ei-ya descended on a trail through an oak-tree-top, and was captured again. When he was brought into camp he found that his favorite son had been killed, in violation of orders, while being held in camp. It was a bitter pill for the old chief to swallow.

For many nights Ten-ei-ya would lift his voice and call, believing that those of his people who were still in the mountains would hear him and come in. But there were no answers to his calls. Once he attempted to escape, and when he was brought before Captain Boling, he expected to be killed. His usual taciturn reserve was broken, and he uttered a pathetic lamentation and a defiant threat, using Indian language interspersed with Spanish words.

"Kill me, Sir Captain! Yes, kill me, as you killed my son; as you would kill my people if they were to come to you! You would kill all my race if you had the power. Yes, Sir American, you can now tell your warriors to kill the old chief; you have made me sorrowful, my life dark; you killed the child of my heart; why not kill the father? But wait a little; when I am dead I will call to my people to come to you, I will call louder than you have had me call; that they shall hear me in their sleep, and come to avenge the death of their chief and his son. Yes, Sir American, my spirit will make trouble for you and your people, as you have caused trouble to me and my people. With the wizards, I will follow the white men and make them fear me. You may kill me, Sir Captain, but you shall not live in peace. I will follow in your footsteps, I will not leave my home, but be with the spirits among the rocks, the waterfalls, in the rivers and in the winds; wheresoever you go I will be with you. You will not see me, but you will fear the spirit of the old chief, and grow cold. The great spirits have spoken! I am done."

Captain Boling's answer was to see that the old chief was fed. Dr. Bunnell, who had reported that he was moved to sympathy and respect for the lordly Ten-ei-ya while he was speaking, remarked that at his food he was "simply a dirty old Indian."

After a second attempt to escape, the proud old chief was tethered by a rope fastened around his waist. With Ten-ei-ya tied to him, Dr. Bunnell explored the high trails in search of Ten-ei-ya's uncaught people. Finally a detachment, taking Ten-ei-ya with them, left the valley on the north cliff trail above Mirror Lake. After reaching the summit, they followed the ridges just below the snow line, to the shores of a lake, now called Tenaya, where they surprised and captured without resistance the remnant of the Yosemites, thirty-five in number, including Ten-ei-ya's four squaws. The young chief of the village, which had so long evaded the pursuing soldiers, declared that he was "not only willing, but anxious" to go to the Commissioners and join in a treaty of peace, for, said he, "Where can we now go that the Americans will not follow us?" and turning to the Captain, "Where can we make our homes that you will not find us?"

On the trip back to the valley, Dr. Bunnell had ample oppor-

tunity to see this marvelous high country not far from the present
Tioga Road which leads from the valley through Tuolumne Meadows to Mono Lake. He maintained that the "sublime mountain
scenery" exceeded any he had ever seen either in Mexico or in the
Rocky Mountains. It was he who suggested that the lake where
the last of the Yosemites had been found be called after Ten-ei-ya.
And so it is called to this day. When Dr. Bunnell told the old chief
of the honor bestowed upon him, Ten-ei-ya protested and said:
"It already has a name; we call it Py-we-ack." It was Dr. Bunnell's
opinion that "the whole mountain region of the water-sheds of the
Merced and Tuolumne Rivers afford the most delightful views to
be seen anywhere of mountain cliffs, cascades and water-falls,
grand forests and mountain meadows." The old chief, Ten-ei-ya,
looking back as they traveled from the lake along the high ridges,
must have felt a similar emotion.

Thus were the Yosemites brought to the camp on the Fresno.
Thus was the Indian war ended.

Major Savage and his friendly Indians re-established their close
relations; but he "never re-visited the valley, and died without
having seen the Vernal and Nevada Falls, or any of the views
belonging to the region of the Yosemite, except those seen from the
valley and from the old Indian trail on our first entrance." In 1852
Major Savage was killed in a controversy with a rival trader in
the Kings, and so, no more of him.

Having accomplished their purpose, the members of the Mariposa Battalion were mustered out of the service, to return to their
various pioneer occupations.

But old Ten-ei-ya, living in the reservation, suffered from the
loss of his dignity and power, claimed that "he could not endure
the heat at the agency, and said that he preferred acorns to the
rations furnished him by the Government." He was granted leave,
and joyfully with his family "took the trail to Yosemite once
more." Later he was joined by other nostalgic members of his band.

After the murder of two prospectors who strayed into the
valley in 1852, a detachment of regular soldiers, under Lieutenant
Moore, captured a party of five of Ten-ei-ya's men who said they
had killed the white men to prevent them from coming into their
valley. The Indians were shot, but, though Lieutenant Moore
crossed the Sierra over the Mono Pass, he failed to find Ten-ei-ya,

for the friendly Monos had received and secreted Ten-ei-ya and his followers. It was said that Ten-ei-ya had been born and had lived among the Monos until his ambition made him a leader and founder of the Pai-ute colony in Ah-wah-nee. Dr. Bunnell has recorded that Ten-ei-ya's "history and warlike exploits formed part of the traditionary lore of the Monos," that "they were proud of his successes and boasted of his descent from their tribe, although Ten-ei-ya, himself, claimed that his father was the chief of an independent people, whose ancestors were of a different race." Dr. Bunnell, in analyzing his character, declared: "Ten-ei-ya had business cunning and sagacity in managing deserters from other tribes, who had sought his protection. He maintained a reputation as a chief whose leadership was never disputed by his followers, and he was the envy of the leaders of other tribes. After his subjection by the whites, he was deserted by his followers, and his supremacy was no longer acknowledged by the neighboring tribes, who had feared rather than respected him or the people of his band."

Ten-ei-ya and his refugee band stayed many moons with the Monos, but finally, according to Dr. Bunnell's account, in the summer of 1853 he and his people returned to their beloved Yosemite Valley, with the intention of remaining there unless they were driven out by the whites. The squaws constructed permanent wigwams near the head of the valley, among the rocks, where they could not easily be seen by visitors. But times may have been hard. At any rate, they made a raid on their friendly relatives, the Monos, and brought back some of the Mono ponies. They were followed into the valley by the indignant Monos, and when sleeping after a feast on horse meat, they were surprised, and sadly enough, Ten-ei-ya was stoned to death. Some of Ten-ei-ya's older men and women were permitted to escape down the valley, but the young men and women were made captives and held as slaves for their captors.

So Ten-ei-ya died, and the valley home he loved so well, after various vicissitudes, is now the famous Yosemite National Park. But that, as Mr. Kipling so often remarked, is another story— a story which will be told in the following pages.

JOHN MUIR AND THE SIERRA NEVADA

"Well may the Sierra be called the Range of Light, not the Snowy Range; for only in winter is it white, while all the year it is bright."
—John Muir, in "Our National Parks," 1901.

ON MARCH 27, 1868, a young Scotch-American, John Muir by name, arrived in San Francisco on the steamer "Nebraska" which had sailed around the Horn, but which he had boarded on the Pacific side of the Isthmus of Panama. With a young Englishman he made straight for the Oakland ferry without giving so much as a glance to the straight rows of buildings on San Francisco's gridiron streets. From Oakland the two young men started on a walking trip which took them down the Santa Clara Valley, across the Pacheco Pass, into the San Joaquin Valley. The scene, as he saw it from the pass, Muir has recorded in his journal:

"Looking down from a height of 1,500 feet, there, extending north and south as far as I could see, lay a vast level flower garden, smooth and level like a lake of gold—the floweriest part of the world I had yet seen. From the eastern margin of the golden plain arose the white Sierra. At the base ran a belt of gently sloping purplish foothills lightly dotted with oaks, above that a broad dark zone of coniferous forests, and above this forest zone arose the lofty mountain peaks, clad in snow. The atmosphere was so clear that although the nearest of the mountain peaks on the axis of the range were at a distance of more than 150 miles, they seemed to be at just the right distance to be seen broadly in their relationship to one another, marshaled in glorious ranks and groups, their snowy robes so smooth and bright that it seemed impossible for a man to walk across the open folds without being seen, even at this distance. Perhaps more than 300 miles of the range was comprehended in this one view."

They crossed the San Joaquin at Hill's Ferry and then followed the Merced toward the Yosemite, which they approached by way of Deer Flat, where the wagon road ended.

The Yosemite was calling to John Muir as a magnet to highly tempered steel. He did not even wait to earn money first, though his pockets had little enough in them. He must see the valley. In this there seems to be something of Fate, for this poor farm boy, born so many miles away in Scotland, had traveled far and incurred much physical discomfort to reach these "mountains of Light," where he spent so many fruitful years of his life, leaving the world richer for his love and learning of the Sierra Nevada Mountains, until his day little known and less understood.

He and his companion spent eight or ten days in the valley, visiting the walls, making sketches, and collecting flowers and ferns. The return trip was made by way of Wawona, where Galen Clark, a Yosemite pioneer, had located. The month in the Yosemite cost John Muir and his friend only three dollars each! Ferns and boughs or the springy forest floor furnished their beds; their shelter, a tree, a cave or the star-lit sky; their food, the scanty provisions they carried in their knapsacks. When they came out of the valley they put their strong young muscles to work in the harvest fields and so earned a small income which more than paid for their Spartan living.

In one of his early journals, Muir recorded: "This Yosemite trip only made me hungry for another far longer and further reaching, and I determined to set out again as soon as I had earned a little money to get near views of the mountains in all their snowy grandeur, and to study the wonderful forests, the noblest of their kind I had ever seen—sugar-pines eight and nine feet in diameter, with cones nearly two feet long, silver firs more than 200 feet in height, Douglas spruce and libocedrus, and the kingly Sequoias."

After spending some time in breaking mustangs, running a ferry, and shearing sheep, he became a sheep-herder in the employ of an Irishman, "Smoky Jack" Connel. On November 1, 1868, he wrote to his friend, Mrs. Carr, whom he had first come to know at the University of Wisconsin before her husband, Professor Carr, came to the University of California: "I am engaged at present in the very important and patriarchal business of sheep. I am a gentle shepherd. The gray box in which I reside is distant about seven miles northwest from Hopeton, two miles north of Snelling's. The Merced pours past me on the south, from the Yosemite; smooth domy hills and the tree fringe of the Tuolumne bound me on the north; the lordly Sierras join sky and plain on the east; and the far coast mountains on the west. My mutton family of 1,800 range over about ten square miles, and I have abundant opportunities for reading and botanizing."

In that charming book, "John of the Mountains," it was recorded by the editor, Mrs. Linnie Marsh Wolfe: "Early in June, 1869, the tall auburn-haired young shepherd John Muir took charge of the sheep of another Irishman, Pat Delaney, and went with them in quest of high green pastures. Assisting him were two dogs and the sub-shepherd Billy, so he had leisure to explore much of the Divide between the Tuolumne and Merced Basins, climb Mount Hoffman and Mount Dana, and penetrate Bloody Canyon to Mono Lake, which lay on the ashen plain 'like a burnished disk.' "

Muir never loved the sheep. He saw the devastation which the "hoofed locusts" were bringing to these enchanted valleys and precious meadows. In the end he fought bitterly to save the best of the high Sierra from destructive grazing.

When Muir returned from this shepherd's expedition, he took up his abode in Yosemite "as a convenient and grand vestibule to the Sierra." He sold the labor of a friend and himself to J. M. Hutchings, a pioneer in the valley, who, through the *California Magazine*, had done much to bring the charms of Yosemite to the public. Hutchings was operating a hotel, and wished to work up some of the down timber into buildings. Muir had had experience in a sawmill in Wisconsin, and so undertook to construct the sawmill. But this work was merely a means to an end. Muir spent as much time as he could on his "observatory," Sentinel Dome. From this and other points of vantage he sought to read the markings on the rocks. He was already developing his theories of glacial action. He wandered into the heights whenever he could. When the summer was over and he was down in the foothills, he determined to spend a winter in the mountains, and so on November 16, 1869, he set out "for Yosemite in particular, and the Sierra in general." He had a companion with him, and in his journal recorded: "I had long lived in bright flowery summer, and I wished to see the snow and ice, the divine jewelry of winter, once more, and to hear the storm-winds among the trees and rocks, and behold the thin azure of the mountains, and their clouds."

On December 6, 1869, Muir wrote to Mrs. Carr: "I am feasting in the Lord's mountain house, and what pen may write my blessings! I am going to dwell here all winter, magnificently 'snow-bound.' Just think of the grandeur of a mountain winter in Yosemite!" Muir remained in the Yosemite through 1870 and into 1871. In

September of 1871 he left the employment of Mr. Hutchings. He had in these years saved enough money to last him, he thought, for years to come, for he dressed in "tough old clothes, gray like the rocks," and could live for months on scanty rations.

Now began in earnest his "glorious toil" with "unmeasured time, and independent of companions and scientific association." Ever since he had arrived at Yosemite in 1868 he had reveled in the beauty of the High Sierra whenever he could make expeditions into the mountains. Now he spent long days and nights in studying the Book of Nature. He evolved and elaborated his theory concerning the creation of Yosemite and other granite valleys in the Sierra. His glacial theory was more daring than it seems today, for he was then a young, unknown man who appeared to many as a vagabond wanderer, only working at anything recognized to be work when he was forced to earn his scanty bread and tea. His theory contradicted the views of some of the most eminent geologists of his day.

John Muir has written many descriptions of Yosemite, at first detailed and fragmentary and later more comprehensive. Long after his life in Yosemite, he gathered together articles he had written for the *Atlantic Monthly* and in 1901 issued a book on "Our National Parks." The descriptions in this book have combined perspective with the first-hand impressions contained in his journals, wherefore a few of his pen pictures are copied here:

"Of all the mountain ranges I have climbed, I like the Sierra Nevada the best. Though extremely rugged, with its main features on the grandest scale in height and depth, it is nevertheless easy of access and hospitable; and its marvelous beauty, displayed in striking and alluring forms, woos the admiring wanderer on and on, higher and higher, charmed and enchanted. Benevolent, solemn, fateful, pervaded with divine light, every landscape glows like a countenance hallowed in eternal repose; and every one of its living creatures, clad in flesh and leaves, and every crystal of its rocks, whether on the surface shining in the sun or buried miles deep in what we call darkness, is throbbing and pulsing with the heartbeats of God. All the world lies warm in one heart, yet the Sierra seems to get more light than other mountains. The weather is mostly sunshine embellished with magnificent storms, and nearly everything shines from base to summit—the rocks, streams, lakes, glaciers, irised falls, and the forests of silver fir and silver pine.

[38]

IN YOSEMITE NATIONAL PARK

ECHO RIDGE ABOVE

Photograph—Marjory Bridge Farquhar

SAWTOOTH RIDGE

Photograph—Ansel Adams
Courtesy—Sierra Club Bulletin

[39]

CATHEDRAL CREEK FALL,
YOSEMITE NATIONAL PARK

Photograph—Marjory Bridge Farquhar

SAWTOOTH RIDGE, MINARETS, OUTSIDE YOSEMITE NATIONAL PARK

Photograph—Walter A. Starr   Courtesy—Sierra Club Bulletin

And how bright is the shining after summer showers and dewy nights, and after frosty nights in spring and autumn, when the morning sunbeams are pouring through the crystals on the bushes and grass, and in winter through the snow-laden trees!

"The average cloudiness for the whole year is perhaps less than ten-hundredths. Scarcely a day of all the summer is dark, though there is no lack of magnificent thundering cumuli. They rise in the warm midday hours, mostly over the middle region, in June and July, like new mountain ranges, higher Sierras, mightily augmenting the grandeur of the scenery while giving rain to the forests and gardens and bringing forth their fragrance. The wonderful weather and beauty inspire everybody to be up and doing. Every summer day is a workday to be confidently counted on, the short dashes of rain forming, not interruptions, but rests. The big blessed storm days of winter, when the whole range stands white, are not a whit less inspiring and kind. Well may the Sierra be called the Range of Light, not the Snowy Range; for only in winter is it white, while all the year it is bright.

"Of this glorious range the Yosemite National Park is a central section, thirty-six miles in length and forty-eight miles in breadth. The famous Yosemite Valley lies in the heart of it, and it includes the head waters of the Tuolumne and Merced Rivers, two of the most songful streams in the world; innumerable lakes and waterfalls and smooth silky lawns; the noblest forests, the loftiest granite domes, the deepest ice-sculptured canyons, the brightest crystalline pavements, and snowy mountains soaring into the sky twelve and thirteen thousand feet, arrayed in open ranks and spiry pinnacled groups partially separated by tremendous canyons and amphitheatres; gardens on their sunny brows, avalanches thundering down their long white slopes, cataracts roaring gray and foaming in the crooked rugged gorges, and glaciers in their shadowy recesses working in silence, slowly completing their sculpture; newborn lakes at their feet, blue and green, free or encumbered with drifting icebergs like miniature Arctic Oceans, shining, sparkling, calm as stars."

Four years before John Muir first saw Yosemite, Congress had in 1864 passed a bill, introduced by Senator Conness, to grant to the State of California "the 'cleft' or 'gorge' in the Granite Peak of the Sierra Nevada Mountains . . . known as the Yo-Semite

Valley, with its branches or spurs" but it was stipulated that the State of California "shall accept this grant upon the express conditions that the premises shall be held for public use, resort, and recreation" and "shall be inalienable for all time." To the State of California also was granted "the tracts embracing what is known as the 'Mariposa Big Tree Grove.'" Here is an Act of Congress, passed eight years before the Yellowstone Act became a law, in which there is a recognition of a public land-use for recreation! Though the act was passed only thirteen years after the first discovery of Yosemite, a number of counter private interests had already grown up.

After the visit of the first tourist party, organized by J. M. Hutchings, accompanied by Thomas Ayres, an artist, in 1855, many people desired to see this wonderland. It was only natural that some sort of accommodation for the public should be undertaken. The land was in the public domain and subject to entry. One homesteader and three who owned hotels or lodges, including Mr. Hutchings, were involved. The Act of Congress made no provision for caring for these private holdings. After prolonged litigation, the courts decided against recognizing the claims, but finally the California State Legislature appropriated $60,000 to recompense the four claimants, and it should be recorded that $5,000 of this appropriation was returned to the State treasury. Thus it was not until 1875 that the Commissioners secured full control of the valley.

The Board of Commissioners appointed by the Governor in 1866 had appointed Galen Clark as guardian of the park, but there were many vicissitudes in the administration of Yosemite, and there was very little money made available to meet the necessary expenses of protecting and administering the park. In 1880 the legislature provided for a new commission. But the criticisms continued.

In the meantime John Muir had begun to publish accounts of Yosemite. On February 5, 1876, he had an article in the Sacramento *Record-Union*, and after that a long line of publications came from his gifted pen. In 1880 Muir married Louie Strenzel, daughter of a pioneer orchardist and horticulturist, and during the succeeding years became an expert orchardist and leading citizen in California.

Through the encouragement of Robert Underwood Johnson, then

Above: THE RITTER
RANGE, FROM IRON
MOUNTAIN.

Photograph—Walter A. Starr

Right: AT THE HEAD OF
SHADOW CREEK,
MT. RITTER AND
BANNER PEAK.

Photograph—Ansel Adams

Below: MINARETS, FROM
THE AIR.

Photograph—Francis P. Farquhar
Courtesy—Sierra Club Bulletin

SUGAR PINES OF YOSEMITE:
SOME WERE SAVED AND
SOME WERE NOT

Photographs—Asahel Curtis and the
Department of the Interior

Courtesy—Portfolio, American Planning
and Civic Association

the editor of the *Century*, Muir began in 1889 to contribute to the magazine. Because Muir saw what was happening to his beloved Sierra country surrounding the Yosemite State Park, he advocated a national park. On October 1, 1890, Congress passed an act withdrawing from settlement all unappropriated lands in the designated public domain, and creating an extensive reservation to be under the exclusive control of the Secretary of the Interior. The act stipulated that the regulations should "provide for the preservation from injury of all timber, mineral deposits, natural curiosities or wonders within said reservation and their retention in their natural condition."

By this time Muir had become convinced that California needed an organization to watch the High Sierra country and help fight the battles which he foresaw would continue to arise. So in 1892, he brought together a group of public-spirited men—William E. Colby, Warren Olney, Sr., Dr. Willis Linn Jepson, and Dr. Joseph LeConte, and they organized the Sierra Club, "to explore, enjoy, and render accessible the mountain regions of the Pacific Coast," "to publish authentic information concerning them," and "to enlist the support and coöperation of the people and government in preserving the forests and other natural features of the Sierra Nevada Mountains." The Club was thus composed of mountain lovers and believers in conservation. The organization has grown in members and power. Through its annual outings, leading to detailed knowledge of the mountains, and the eminence of many of its members, the Club has been in a position to exercise a potent influence in legislative and administrative policies concerning the Sierra.

One of the first beneficial undertakings of the Club was to seek to bring about the recession to the Federal Government of the Yosemite State Park. Even under favorable circumstances it was an anomaly that the Federal Government should administer a rim of land around a core, set aside for the very same purpose, under the administration of the State. Then, as now, when the proposal was made to return to the Federal Government land which it had given to the State, there was bitter local opposition, especially in the county seats of the four nearby counties.

After the creation of the national park in 1890, Congress was slow in providing funds for administration. So the Department of the Interior called upon the War Department, as it had done in Yellowstone, and for twenty-three years the park was patrolled and protected by the Army.

While the four claimants in the floor of the valley had been compensated by the State, there were in the national park many private holdings which the Federal Government did not buy. This necessitated boundary changes, and the pressure was very great to take out of the park any land in which there might be potential mining values. In 1904 General Hiram Chittenden, known through his Yellowstone book, published in 1895 (see page 19), became chairman of a boundary commission, which agreed to eliminate from the national park large areas on the east and west. In 1906 a tract on the southwest was cut out of the park. Today many believe that some areas, not yet restored through the purchases of recent years, should be added to Yosemite, notably the lofty Minarets and stately Mt. Ritter, with their surrounding frame of high mountain peaks. Muir's journals of the seventies contained fascinating and detailed descriptions of this region.

From the South Fork of the San Joaquin Canyon he once recorded: "View very grand and universal. Ritter the noblest and most ornate of all." On a trip to the Minarets, he remarked: "The Minarets were now fairly within my grasp. I had been crossing canyons for five days. . . . Their appearance from here was impressively sublime because of their great height, narrow bases, linear arrangement and dark color. They are the most elaborately carved on the edges of any slate summits I have seen. Four lakes lie like open eyes below the ample clouds of névé that send them water. These névé slopes are large, and wonderfully adapted in form and situation for picturesque effects among the black angular slate slabs and peaks."

And again: "At the foot of a former moraine of this west glacier is a small lake not one hundred yards long, but grandly framed with a sheer wall of névé twenty feet high. . . . Beautiful caves reached back from the water's edge; in some places granite walls overleaned and big blocks broke off from the main névé wall, and, with angles sharp as those of ice, leaned into the lake. Undermined by the water, the fissures filled with blue light, and water dripped and trickled all along the white walls. The sun was shining. I never saw so grand a setting for a glacier lake. The

[46]

sharp peaks of Ritter seen over the snow shone with splendid effect." Who can doubt that the highest use of this spectacular mountain region is that of a national park?

So long as he lived, John Muir did much to direct public interest to, and provide guardianship for, the High Sierra country. In many instances he succeeded, though it is well recognized today that some of the compromises forced upon the friends of the national parks should be remedied so far as this is yet possible.

The closing years of John Muir's life were darkened by the unsuccessful fight he and the Sierra Club made to save Hetch Hetchy from being turned into a reservoir. In this fight he was ably seconded by Dr. J. Horace McFarland, then President of the American Civic Association.

But in spite of all that the friends of Yosemite National Park could do, Congress in 1913 passed an act to permit the City of San Francisco to build a reservoir in Hetch Hetchy—a yosemite second in beauty only to the big Yosemite. No one dreamed at that time that within twenty-five years the Yosemite Valley would be so crowded with summer visitors that its very charm and beauty are threatened and that Hetch Hetchy would be sorely needed by its joint owners, the people of the United States, for the purpose to which it was dedicated when Yosemite National Park was created: "public use, resort, and recreation." But even then it was realized that the water flowed out of the park and that it was not a *waste* of water to permit the park waters to ripple down the floor of the valley to places where they could be impounded at possibly greater expense. It was not essentially a question of apportionment of waters. It was a question of money. The sacrifice of this exquisite valley was exacted, not to provide water for the people of San Francisco, but to save them money. John Muir and his associates knew then that the valley should have been held inviolate, and we recognize today as never before, the importance of protecting our national parks. Hetch Hetchy remains a horrible example of a disastrous mistake, which failed to save money.

The military regime in Yosemite came to an end in connection with the creation of the National Park Service by Act of Congress in 1916, following the initial proposal by Dr. J. Horace McFarland. The Sierra Club supported the movement. Mr. Muir died in 1914, soon after Congress authorized the Hetch Hetchy desecration.

In the years since then, Yosemite has been served well by three superintendents—W. B. Lewis and Colonel C. G. Thomson, now deceased, and the present incumbent, Lawrence Merriam.

During all this time, the park administrators have been harassed by private land holdings within the park and by too closely drawn boundaries. The most menacing holdings were tracts of timber within the park and on its border held by companies ready to begin cutting or actually harvesting their tree crop. In 1930, the park was put in a position to purchase over 10,000 acres of land at a cost in excess of $3,000,000, half of which was met by John D. Rockefeller, Jr. Following legislation and appropriation of funds by Congress in 1937, nearly 8,000 acres of sugar pines near the Big Oak Flat Road were acquired, at a cost in excess of a million and a half, though the summer before the purchase was actually made, the lumber companies put as many men as they could work into the area and wrought a terrible devastation.

Much as Muir loved Yosemite, no one can read his voluminous writings, many of them published through the devoted service of Dr. William F. Badé, his literary executor, and not be impressed with his love and knowledge of the entire Sierra Nevada.

Muir first visited the Big Trees in 1875. He was not the discoverer of these trees. They were first seen by white man in 1858 when Hale Tharp, a pioneer who had settled on a ranch about two and a half miles below Three Rivers in 1856, made a trip to what we now know as Giant Forest. Tharp reported that there were about 2,000 Indians then living along the Kaweah Rivers.

It will be remembered that the famous Mariposa Battalion divided its forces—that while two companies were scouring the Yosemite, another company under Captain Kuykendall went south to bring in the Indians on the Kaweah. Captain Kuykendall, according to Dr. Bunnell's account, "vigorously operated in the valleys, hills and mountains of the Kings and Kaweah Rivers and those of the smaller streams south. The Indians of the Kern River, owing to the influence of a Mission chief, 'Don Vicente,' who had a plantation at the Tejon Pass, remained peaceable, and were not disturbed. The success of Captain Kuykendall's campaigns enabled the Commissioners to make treaties with all the tribes within the Tulare Valley, and those that occupied the region south of the

Above: CREST OF THE SIERRA, MT. SILL
AND RIDGE NEAR MIDDLE PALISADE

Photograph—Ansel Adams

Right: JOHN MUIR SHELTER AT
MUIR PASS

Photograph—Marjory Bridge Farquhar
Courtesy—Sierra Club Bulletin

Below: MT. CLARENCE KING

Photograph—Ansel Adams
Courtesy—American Planning and Civic Annual

LITTLE PETE MEADOW AND
LANGILLE PEAK

Photograph—Herbert P. Rankin

ON THE JOHN MUIR TRAIL

EVOLUTION CREEK

Photograph—Ansel Adams
Courtesy—Sierra Club Bulletin

San Joaquin River." After an encounter on the Kings River, the Indians in alarm fled into the canyons. It was while pursuing the fugitives that Captain Kuykendall saw some of the country which he said "was simply indescribable." The stories of the South Sierra brought back by the Captain and his men "were received with doubts or as exaggerations." They declared that they had seen deeper valleys and higher cliffs than were described by those who visited Yosemite. One of the soldiers who afterwards visited Yosemite declared: "The Kings River country, and the territory southeast of it, beats the Yosemite in terrific grandeur, but in sublime beauty you have got us."

The Kings River had been discovered by an early Spanish explorer who crossed the river on Epiphany Sunday, 1805, and named it "Rio de los Sanctos Reyes"—River of the Holy Kings.

Apparently none of the Mariposa Battalion caught a glimpse of the Big Trees of the South Sierra. That discovery was reserved for Hale Tharp some eight years after the military visit to the Canyons of the Kaweahs. That story has been told in the book on the "Big Trees," written by Walter Fry, United States Commissioner, and John R. White, then Superintendent of Sequoia National Park. Mr. Tharp was quoted: "During the summer of 1858, accompanied by two Indians, I made my first trip into the Giant Forest. We went in by way of the Middle Fork River and Moro Rock, and camped a few days at Log Meadow, and came out by the same route. . . . I had two objects in making the trip. One was for the purpose of locating a high summer range for my stock, and the other was due to the fact that stories the Indians had told me of the 'big tree' forest caused me to wonder, so I decided to go and see." Said Mr. Tharp: "I made my second exploration trip into the Giant Forest during the summer of 1860. . . . I took with me John Swanson. We camped one night at Log Meadow, then went on over into the Kings River Canyon, returning again to Log Meadow after a period of about two weeks. . . . So far as I am aware, I am the first white man who ever visited either the Sequoia National Park or the Three Rivers region."

In the spring of 1861 Mr. Tharp began to occupy the Giant Forest as a summer range for stock. He reported that "We saw hundreds of deer, grouse, quail, and a few bear on our trip. We also saw six of the mountain gray wolves." Mr. Tharp recalled that "from 1861 to 1890, when the park was created, I held the Giant Forest country as my range, and some of my family went there every year with the stock. When the land up there was thrown on the market, with other men we bought large holdings." Hale Tharp's summer home at Giant Forest consisted of a huge hollow sequoia log fitted with door, window, and stone fireplace. Messrs. Fry and White have described this fallen tree as 24 feet in diameter at the butt and have estimated its height to have been 311 feet when it fell. This house-in-a-log is now carefully preserved by the National Park Service as one of the antiquities of the park.

It was in 1879 that John Muir was reported to have visited Hale Tharp at Log Meadow, though Muir made his first trip to the Kings and the Big Trees in 1875. It was in 1873 that Muir's Journals carried entries of his climb up Mt. Whitney from the east.

Muir's 1875 trip, as recorded in his book on "Our National Parks," must have been a real adventure. He took with him a "little Brownie mule," but reported that "many a time in the course of our journey when he was jaded and hungry, wedged fast in rocks or struggling in chaparral like a fly in a spiderweb, his troubles were sad to see, and I wished he would leave me and find his way home." Muir told in his book, "I struck out into the majestic trackless forest to the southeastward (from Mariposa Grove), hoping to find new groves or traces of old ones in the dense silver fir and pine woods about the head of Big Creek, where soil and climate seemed most favorable to their growth, but not a single tree or old monument of any sort came to light until I climbed the high rock called Wamellow by the Indians. Here I obtained telling views of the fertile forest-filled basin of the Upper Fresno. Innumerable spires of the noble yellow pine were displayed rising above one another on the braided slopes, and yet nobler sugar pines with superb arms outstretched in the rich autumn light, while away toward the southwest, on the verge of the glowing horizon, I discovered the majestic dome-like crowns of Big Trees towering high over all, singly and in close grove congregations. There is something wonderfully attractive in this king tree, even when beheld from afar, that draws us to it with indescribable enthusiasm; its superior height and massive smoothly rounded outlines proclaiming its character in any company; and when one of the oldest attains full stature on some commanding ridge it seems the very god of the woods."

While Muir declared that "no description can give any adequate idea of their singular majesty, much less of their beauty," yet he has left us some of the best descriptions anywhere to be found. He wrote: "Excepting the sugar pine, most of their neighbors with pointed tops seem to be forever shouting Excelsior, while the Big Tree, though soaring above them all, seems satisfied, its rounded head, poised lightly as a cloud, giving no impression of trying to go higher. Only in youth does it show like other conifers a heaven-ward yearning, keenly aspiring with a long quick-growing top. Indeed the whole tree for the first century or two, or until a hundred to a hundred and fifty feet high, is arrowhead in form, and, compared with the solemn rigidity of age, is as sensitive to the wind as a squirrel tail. The lower branches are gradually dropped as it grows older, and the upper ones thinned out until comparatively few are left. These, however, are developed to great size, divide again and again, and terminate in bossy rounded masses of leafy branchlets, while the head becomes dome-shaped. . . .

"Perfect specimens, unhurt by running fires or lightning, are singularly regular and symmetrical in general form, though not at all conventional, showing infinite variety in sure unity and harmony of plan. The immensely strong, stately shafts, with rich purplish brown bark, are free of limbs for a hundred and fifty feet or so, though dense tufts of sprays occur here and there, producing an ornamental effect, while long parallel furrows give a fluted columnar appearance. . . . A particularly knotty, angular, ungovernable-looking branch, five to eight feet in diameter and perhaps a thousand years old, may occasionally be seen pushing out from the trunk as if determined to break across the bounds of the regular curve, but like all the others, as soon as the general outline is approached the huge limb dissolves into massy bosses of branchlets and sprays, as if the tree were growing beneath an invisible bell glass against the sides of which the branches were moulded, while many small, varied departures from the ideal form give the impression of freedom to grow as they like.

"Except in picturesque old age, after being struck by lightning and broken by a thousand snowstorms, this regularity of form is one of the Big Tree's most distinguishing characteristics. Another is the simple sculptural beauty of the trunk and its great thickness as compared with its height and the width of the branches, many of them being from eight to ten feet in diameter at a height of two hundred feet from the ground, and seeming more like finely modeled and sculptured architectural columns than the stems of trees, while the great strong limbs are like rafters supporting the magnificent dome head. . . .

"The bark of full grown trees is from one to two feet thick, rich cinnamon brown, purplish on young trees and shady parts of the old, forming magnificent masses of color with the underbrush and beds of flowers. . . .

"The cones are bright grass-green in color, about two and a half inches long, one and a half wide, and are made up of thirty or forty strong, closely packed, rhomboidal scales with four to eight seeds at the base of each. The seeds are extremely small and light. . . .

"The faint lisp of snowflakes as they alight is one of the smallest sounds mortal can hear. The sound of falling sequoia seeds, even when they happen to strike on flat leaves or flakes of bark, is about as faint. Very different is the bumping and thudding of the falling cones. . . .

"The Big Tree keeps its youth far longer than any of its neighbors. Most silver firs are old in their second or third century, pines in their fourth or fifth, while the Big Tree growing beside them is still in the bloom of its youth, juvenile in every feature at the age of old pines, and cannot be said to attain anything like prime size and beauty before its fifteen hundredth year, or under favorable circumstances become old before its three thousandth. . . .

"It is a curious fact that all the very old sequoias have lost their heads by lightning. . . . But of all living things sequoia is perhaps the only one able to wait long enough to make sure of being struck by lightning. Thousands of years it stands ready and waiting, offering its head to every passing cloud as if inviting its fate, praying for heaven's fire as a blessing; and when at last the old head is off, another of the same shape immediately begins to grow on. Every bud and branch seems excited, like bees that have lost their queen, and tries hard to repair the damage. Branches that for many centuries have been growing out horizontally at

[54]

FALLS IN UPPER PALISADE
CANYON

ON THE JOHN MUIR TRAIL

DEVILS CRAGS FROM PALISADE CREEK

Photographs—Ansel Adams   Courtesy—Sierra Club Bulletin

KINGS RIVER
CANYON

Left: NORTH TOWER,
FROM TALUS SLOPE OF
GLACIER MONUMENT

Right: PARADISE PEAK,
LOOKING EAST FROM
SLOPES AT FOOT OF
HELMET

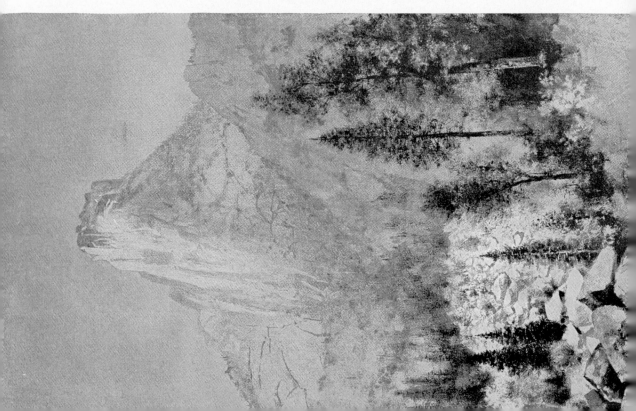

once turn upward, and all their branchlets arrange themselves with reference to a new top of the same peculiar curve as the old one. Even the small subordinate branches halfway down the trunk do their best to push up to the top and help in this curious head-making.''

Like all of Muir's descriptions these words reveal not only what he saw in a single contemplation but what he had observed over a long period of years. He knew the inner life of the sequoias as well as the face they turned toward the world.

Muir's writings, which began to appear in the late seventies, carried news of these impressive giant trees to the reading world, but it was as a result of local effort that the first legislation was proposed to protect these helpless giants which could be hacked down, even with the crude tools then in use, though many of the huge trees which were cut have never been removed from their graves and no one was the gainer. As in the case of many other fine movements there were several sources of information and action. Articles began to appear in the Visalia *Delta* in 1879. The first sawmills, according to Messrs. Fry and White, were about fifty miles east of Visalia, near what is now General Grant National Park. At the same time the California Academy of Sciences was already working for the creation of a liberal Sequoia National Park to embrace a great area in the Sierra between Sequoia and Yosemite. But in a letter to Colonel John R. White, dated June 8, 1929, Colonel George W. Stewart of Visalia, who was largely responsible for the long-continued effort to save the Sequoia country, told of the beginnings of the movement in Visalia. It seems that in 1879, Tipton Lindsey, Receiver of the United States Land Office at Visalia, suggested to J. D. Hyde, Register of the Land Office, that they make an attempt to have the General Grant Grove, then known as the Fresno-Tulare Grove, suspended from entry. As a result, the United States Surveyor-General at San Francisco, Theodore Wagner, formerly a resident of Visalia, issued an order suspending the four sections in which it was thought these trees were located. Later the order of suspension was amended to include the land now in General Grant National Park.

In December of 1881, Senator John F. Miller, who was familiar with the articles in the *Delta*, and had kept in sympathetic touch with the movement, introduced a bill into Congress to create a "national park of the whole west flank of the Sierra Nevada from Tehipite to a point southeast of Porterville and from the higher foothills eastward to the summit of the range." The bill was never reported out of committee because of the objections of the local residents.

Colonel Stewart, who had been absent in Hawaii for three years, again joined the *Delta* when he returned to Visalia. In his 1929 letter to Colonel White, he told of the case of three men who attempted to get possession of Giant Forest and surrounding timber by having a number of men from the Bay region apply for a quarter section of land each under the Timber and Stone Law, but the applications were suspended by the Land Office and the suspension was never revoked. Otherwise, no doubt, the Giant Forest would have fallen as other fine Big Trees fell before the crude cutting tools of the lumbermen, though, due to damages in felling, difficulties in "working" the lumber into useful shape and transporting it, there was always a high percentage of waste and often total loss.

The story recounted by Colonel Stewart in his letter to Colonel White cleared up a number of obscure points, and has given us an authentic record of what happened nearly fifty years ago to save the Big Trees for this and future generations. It is inconceivable that civilized America should now ever withdraw its solemn dedication of the Sequoia country to the enjoyment of the people. Colonel Stewart's account is that of an actor in the play. He wrote:

"At that time we had many editorials and special articles on forest fires, timber trespasses, the saving of the big trees, and kindred topics and were in the habit of sending marked copies of the *Delta* or clippings from its columns to the Secretary of the Interior. Later in 1885, in November, I believe, the Secretary suspended eighteen townships of mountain land from entry because of alleged incorrect surveys. The suspended area covered all, or practically all, of the sequoia groves on the public lands in Fresno and Tulare counties.

"In 1889 a meeting of Tulare County citizens held at Visalia adopted a resolution favoring the creation of a forest reserve to embrace a territory to be named later, and the meeting adjourned to meet later in Fresno. We went to that meeting with the suggested boundaries prepared, the same taking in the entire forest region from Yosemite (State) Park to some point in Kern County. The

Fresno meeting approved the idea, and the first petition naming a large and definite area for a forest reserve was sent to Washington before there was any law therefor.

"Some time that year or early in 1890 . . . the Secretary of the Interior revoked the suspension of 1885 as to the township in which the Atwell mill is situated. . . . Four of us wired a protest to Washington and followed this with a numerously signed petition, and the Secretary rescinded his order revoking the suspension.

"A few weeks later there were current rumors that the Giant Forest region was to be opened to entry. We then began to realize that a mere suspension of lands from entry was not a very efficient protection with a man like Noble at the head of the Department.

"It was then that we thought of the Yellowstone National Park, and read the act creating it and decided that only a national park would insure the permanent preservation of the Giant Forest and other big tree groves.

"I was editor and publisher of the *Delta* at that time. Mr. F. J. Walker, who had been an employee and later a publisher of the paper, was then not otherwise engaged and devoted about three months of his time to helping me on the *Delta*, and especially for the purpose of making this fight for the Forest. We took the matter up with General Vandever, member of Congress from our District, who at once became interested and introduced the bill.

"We wrote letters to every person in the United States, in and out of Congress, whom we knew to . . . favor the idea. Their name was not legion in those days. The response, with few exceptions, was cordial. The one in the East who was head and shoulders above all others in the good work was the editor of *Forest and Stream*, and he interested a number of influential persons and organizations there. . . . We desired to have a large park, embracing Mount Whitney, the Kings and Kern rivers, and the big tree areas, but under the circumstances thought it inadvisable to attempt so much. We had some difficulty in convincing others that it was not an opportune time to ask for so much, and we deemed the proper course to be to confine our efforts to saving the big trees, then in immediate danger. The river canyons we thought could be added if we once had a park in existence. We didn't think then the enlargement of the park would be so long deferred. . . .

"The creation of General Grant National Park was due to the timely suggestion of D. K. Zumwalt of Visalia at the psychological moment. Several people had been interested in the preservation of that area, but Mr. Zumwalt happened to be in Washington at the time the enlargement of Sequoia and the creation of Yosemite Park was up for passage, and his recommendation that the General Grant Grove be also made a park was acted upon favorably by General Vandever and by Congress."

But the hopes of Colonel Stewart and his friends who persuaded their enthusiastic supporters to accept half a loaf were to be long deferred. After the Acts of Congress of 1890, John Muir immediately set himself to work for the enlargement of Sequoia National Park to include Mt. Whitney, the Kern and Kings country. In an article in the *Century Magazine* in November, 1891, entitled, "A Rival to the Yosemite, the Canyon of the South Fork of the King's River, California," Muir presented to the American public the most remarkable descriptions of the Kings country which are extant. He wrote:

"The bottom of the valley is about 5,000 feet above the sea, and its level or gently sloping surface is diversified with flowery meadows and groves and open sunny flats, through the midst of which the crystal river, ever changing, ever beautiful, makes its way; now gliding softly with scarce a ripple over beds of brown pebbles, now rushing and leaping in wild exultation across avalanche rock-dams or terminal moraines, swaying from side to side, beaten with sunshine, or embowered with leaning pines and firs, alders, willows, and tall balsam poplars, which with the bushes and grass at their feet make charming banks. Gnarled snags and stumps here and there reach out from the banks, making cover for trout which seem to have caught their colors from rainbow spray, though hiding mostly in shadows, where the current swirls slowly and protecting sedges and willows dip their leaves.

"From this long, flowery, forested, well-watered park the walls rise abruptly in plain precipices or richly sculptured masses partly separated by side canyons, displaying wonderful wealth and variety of architectural forms, which are as wonderful in beauty of color and fineness of finish as in colossal height and mass. The so-called war of the elements has done them no harm. There is no unsightly defacement as yet; deep in the sky, inviting the onset of

KINGS RIVER CANYON.
PART OF SOUTH WALL OF
TEHIPITE VALLEY

Original drawing by Charles D. Robinson, who
accompanied John Muir on his trip in 1891. Repro-
duced from plates in Century Magazine by permission
of D. Appleton-Century Co.

Courtesy—Planning and Civic Comment

THE SPHINX,
OVERLOOKING THE KINGS CANYON

Photograph—Anse' Adams
Courtesy—Sierra Club Bulletin

[61]

Photograph—Ansel Adams   Courtesy—Portfolio, American Planning and Civic Association

THE ROARING CASCADES OF THE KINGS RIVER

[62]

storms through unnumbered centuries, they will stand firm and
seemingly as fresh and unworn as new-born flowers. . . .

"When from some commanding summit we view the mighty
wilderness about this central valley, and, after tracing its tributary
streams, note how every converging canyon shows in its sculpture,
moraines and shining surfaces that it was once the channel of a
glacier, contemplating this dark period of grinding ice, it would
seem that here was a center of storm and stress to which no life
would come. But it is just where the ancient glaciers bore down
on the mountain flank with crushing and destructive and most
concentrated energy that the most impressive displays of divine
beauty are offered to our admiration. Even now the snow falls
every winter about the valley to a depth of ten to twenty feet,
and the booming of avalanches is a common sound. Nevertheless
the frailest flowers, blue and gold and purple, bloom on the brows
of the great canyon rocks, and on the frosty peaks, up to a height of
13,000 feet, as well as in sheltered hollows and on level meadows
and lake borders and banks of streams."

Muir described the charming Paradise Valley and the "spacious
and enchantingly beautiful" Tehipite Valley. He crossed the
divide to the Middle Fork of the Kings by way of Copper Creek
to this valley, about three miles long and half a mile wide, with
walls from 2,500 to nearly 4,000 feet in height. He found the famous
Tehipite Dome "sublimely simple and massive in structure," "one
of the most striking and wonderful rocks in the Sierra." There
were detailed descriptions of scores of marvelous peaks, the Sphinx,
"one of the most remarkable in the Sierra," Cathedral Rocks,
"most elaborately sculptured, and the most beautiful series of
rocks . . . seen in any yosemite in the range," Glacier Monument, "the broadest, loftiest, and most sublimely beautiful of all
these wonderful rocks," the North Tower, "a square, boldly
sculptured mass 2,000 feet in height," the Dome arches, "heavily
glaciated, and offering telling sections of domed and folded structure," and many others.

Muir made a number of trips to the Mt. Whitney-Kings-
Kern country. He must many times have traversed the Sierra
crests south of Yosemite. His name today is attached to a grove
of Big Trees on the Kaweah River in Sequoia National Park, to
the Muir Woods of *Sequoia sempervirens* in the shadow of Mt.

Tamalpais, to a mountain in the High Sierra, to an incomparable Pass, and to the John Muir Trail of nearly 200 miles, as measured in the guide book of Walter A. Starr, Jr., published posthumously in 1934. But though there are these memorials to John Muir, much of the superlatively fine region he passionately desired to see in the National Park System still remains outside, some of it injured beyond repair, some of it capable of being restored to its wilderness state, some of it threatened with future destruction, but much of it, mercifully, still waiting for its crown of kingdom which would be bestowed by declaring it forever immune to commercial exploitation and for all time preserved for the people.

It was twelve years after the death of John Muir before the Mt. Whitney and the Kern regions were added to Sequoia National Park, and that addition was the result of an unwilling, but seemingly inevitable, compromise on the part of those who were fighting for a larger area, including the Kings country. Twenty-five years ago, John Muir died, confidently expecting that the Kings canyons, about which he wrote so eloquently in 1891, twenty-two years before, would be given national-park status.

The fine service which John Muir rendered to the American people in acquainting them with the intimate life of the Sierra Nevada through unrivaled descriptions and first-hand information, can never be measured. For John Muir not only *saw* and *felt* his scenery, but he spent days and years studying the Book of Nature in the Sierra so that he could *read* and *interpret* its story to the world. It was he who discovered the traces of the great glaciers which carved the yosemites of the Sierra. He knew its trees, its flowers and shrubs. He knew the animals which roamed its mountain fastnesses. He knew its weather and its habits of flood and storm. He knew its sunshine.

It seems incredible that this act to place the Kings canyons and high surrounding Sierra in the national-park category of land-use should have been so long delayed.

DR. McFARLAND AND THE NATIONAL PARK SYSTEM

"Nowhere in official Washington can an inquirer find an office of the National Parks, or a desk devoted solely to their management."
—Dr. J. Horace McFarland, Annual Convention,
American Civic Association, Washington, December, 1911

IN 1890 the United States had four national parks, created through the unselfish devotion of a few public-spirited citizens who had the vision to see into the future and try to avert the disastrous results of excessive commercial exploitation of our lands and waters. So far no one had promulgated the idea of a National Park System. There were signs, however, that sporadic thinking and acting would bring into being enough of these new land-use areas to create a new category or class.

In 1890 visitors to Yellowstone or Yosemite traveled to certain railheads—the outposts of civilization—and then were transported by stage into the parks. If they penetrated beyond the rather rough wagon roads, they were obliged to walk or ride horseback. Who could have dreamed that a day would arrive when nearly thirty million automobiles would be distributed at the rate of one for every four people in the United States? What would our hard-working New England ancestors have thought of the vacation trips of the twenties, of the thousands of miles of hard pavements which were to follow 1916?

In 1893 a bill was introduced into Congress by Senator Watson C. Squire to create the Washington National Park, to include the spectacularly majestic Mt. Rainier, but it was not until March 2, 1899, in President McKinley's administration, that Mt. Rainier, with its ancient glaciers lying deep and its pristine snowy robe re-newed each year, with its trailing glory of forests and streams, was created a national park. The four national parks which had been cre-ated up to this time were taken from the public domain. Mt. Rainier National Park was set aside from the "Pacific Forest Re-serve." That is, it had already been removed from the public domain and placed in the forest-reserve class. These forest reserves, later to become "national forests," were an evidence that the conservation idea was beginning to take hold. Today the far-flung national forests bear eloquent testimony to the vision of those who have, through the years, promoted this form of land-use. But, with Yellowstone,

[65]

Yosemite, Sequoia, and General Grant leading the way, it was already becoming apparent that there were these two separate and distinct forms of public land-use, besides others which were coming to be recognized. At first Rainier was not adequately protected against mineral claims but in 1908 an amendment prohibited the location of new mining claims in the park, although the old ones were protected. In Mt. Rainier National Park, as in most of the other national parks, except Yellowstone, private rights had already been established, but the act of dedication provided that settler- and railroad-owned lands could be exchanged for lieu lands in order to clear the title to the park. The American people gave land away with a free hand, and then, when it was discovered that they had been mistaken, the lands were often bought back, sometimes with the grant of other lands and sometimes for cash from the public treasury. This process, however unprofitable, worked little harm where the lands themselves were not damaged. Unfortunately, the granted lands which bore some of the finest forests of the New World came back to the ownership of the people shorn of their glory and without much economic value. The extent of erosion-control of this era is one indication that lands which once were assets have become actual liabilities.

And so Mt. Rainier, with an all too scanty rim of protection, became a national park. It could hardly be said that even yet we were consciously working for a National Park System. When the twentieth century dawned, twenty-eight years after the establishment of Yellowstone National Park, we had but five national parks in three States. But in 1902 Crater Lake, with its icy waters of sapphire blue, became a national park. It was reserved from the public lands in the State of Oregon, "set apart forever as a public park or pleasure ground for the benefit of the people of the United States," and assigned to the Secretary of the Interior for control and custody. The act expressly forbade "all residence and settlement and the engaging in business or speculative enterprises," but the park was to be open to "scientists, excursionists and pleasure seekers," *and* to the locating and working of mining claims, a menace which has been removed from many of the existing parks but which still hangs like a dark cloud over projects for parks-to-be. We are a metal-hungry people, and in spite of over-production of certain metals and the uneconomic expense of operation for the mining of others, we still think that the impecunious should be permitted to "prospect" for wealth. Apparently we still have faith in Aladdin's lamp, rather than a sound economic system which will permit our people to become and remain joint owners of inspiring natural-scenic areas, safe from economic exploitation.

The Crater Lake Act mentioned specifically what was perhaps implicit in the original Yellowstone Act, and that is the invitation to scientists to come to the park. It was a good many years before we were to undertake seriously a program of education and science in the national parks, but it was coming, and here, thirty-five years ago, in the Crater Lake Act, was a recognition of its desirability.

We then had six national parks, all areas of indisputable beauty and national interest; all of them, except Yellowstone, spotted with private rights and easements which were long to trouble their administrators and limit their service to the public. The promoters of these national parks had vision, but they were obliged to make concessions to the commercial demands of the times. Public opinion was not yet sufficiently informed or possessed of that firm conviction which is needed to resist the pressure of local business interests. But the idea of national parks was growing, and as visitors increased year by year, the education of the American people was being carried on. The time was coming when the people would unite to protect their joint property from harmful encroachments—at first not always successfully, but who can doubt the ultimate outcome?

In 1903 Wind Cave National Park was created in South Dakota. Wind Cave is an interesting phenomenon, but in the light of later discoveries of larger and more impressive caves, it may be that its correct classification would bring it into the State Park System, to be administered in connection with the highly scenic Custer State Park, only a few miles north of it. Possibly it should have been a national monument, a land status which at the time of the Wind Cave Act had not yet been defined.

In 1902 the Secretary of the Interior was charged with the administration of mineral springs in the Chickasaw Indian territory. In 1906, when Oklahoma became a State, the sulphur springs were designated as Platt National Park. This was reminis-

cent of the Hot Springs, in Arkansas, much visited for their cura-
tive waters, which had been a public reservation since 1832. It was
awarded to the National Park Service in the Act of 1916, and
finally became a national park in 1921. (There is some question,
perhaps, as to whether a better classification and a more appropriate agency to administer these springs might be found.)

In 1906 Congress passed an Act for the Preservation of American
Antiquities, which authorized the President by proclamation to
set aside lands owned or controlled by the United States, containing "historic landmarks, historic or prehistoric structures
and other objects of historic or prehistoric interest," as national
monuments. Some fault has been found with the term "monument." To some critics it has unpleasant connotations. But so
far no one has been able to think of any more descriptive or appropriate title. It has now been in common use in the United States,
recognized by the law, for more than thirty years, and has come
to have a meaning of its own.

Honorable John F. Lacey, Congressman from Iowa, who had
taken the lead in securing passage of the Antiquities Act, also
sponsored the bill to create Mesa Verde National Park which
became a law three weeks after the approval of the Antiquities
Act. Except for the fact that the reservation was created by stat-
ute instead of by Executive Order, there seems no reason why Mesa
Verde, one of the most extensive and alluring archeological areas
in the United States, should not be a national monument, for its
scenery, though impressive, would hardly entitle it to become a
national park. Perhaps the difficulty has been that many have
thought of national monuments as less important than national
parks. This is not the case. From an archeological or scientific
point of view, they may be much more important.

In this little chronological account of how the national parks
and monuments came into existence, piecemeal, without comprehensive plan, it is clear, for the most part, that the period was
characterized by *laissez-faire*—"let it alone," or "let it happen"
as it may. Then in 1908 came an event of great significance.
President Theodore Roosevelt called a Conservation Conference
of Governors in Washington, and to this he invited public officials,
university presidents, and officers of the leading conservation
organizations. The Conference was called to give direction and

impetus to the then comparatively new conservation of our forests, which many realized were fast disappearing from the surface of our land. President Roosevelt also had in mind a broader program of conservation to include lands, waters, and minerals. The proceedings of that Conference, three inches thick, stand on the library shelves today. One may look through these five hundred odd pages and find many useful suggestions for the conservation of our natural resources and our economic assets. Speakers from California, Washington, Colorado, and Wyoming, where there were scenic assets recognized by the entire Nation, made no mention of conservation as applied to these precious possessions. In over 200,000 words not over 2,000 were devoted to conservation of natural scenery. Dr. McFarland shared with Governor Charles Evans Hughes of New York the honor of directing the attention of the Conference to this important subject.

Dr. McFarland urged consideration of "one of America's greatest resources—her unmatched natural scenery." Said he: "The National Parks, all too few in number and extent, ought to be held absolutely inviolate as intended by Congress. . . . The scenic value of all the national domain yet remaining should be jealously guarded as a distinctly important national resource, and not as a mere incidental increment. . . . We have for a century, Mr. Chairman, stood actually, if not ostensibly, for an uglier America; let us here and now resolve, for every patriotic and economic reason, to stand openly and solidly for a more beautiful, and therefore a more prosperous America!"

The high note of Governor Hughes' address was a sentence which indicated his sentiments: "The conservation of our resources means not merely their physical preservation but their safeguarding of the common interest in the beauties of nature and their protection both from the ruthless hand of the destroyer and from the grasp of selfish interest." Governor Hughes recounted as an important part of the achievements of the great State of New York the setting aside of the Adirondack Forest Park.

These fine sentiments earned in the thousand-word resolutions adopted by the Governors exactly one word, which indicated that among the desirable effects of conservation of natural resources "the *beauty*, healthfulness, and habitability of our country should be preserved and increased."

But the words of Dr. McFarland, though they may have fallen on ears attuned only to the conservation and utilization of material resources, acted as a spur to himself. From the time of the Conference, he put the force of his dynamic personality behind the movement to secure a single agency in the United States Government which should be responsible for protecting and administering the national parks. He began to envision a system. The first step was to secure the agency. In the eight years during which there were pending measures before Congress to establish such an agency, Glacier, Rocky Mountain, Hawaii, and Lassen National Parks were created, and a number of national monuments were set aside by Executive Order of the President.

Glacier National Park, embracing some of the finest of the northern Rocky Mountains, streaked with living glaciers and spotted with glacial lakes, comprising a long section of the Continental Divide, covered 1,500 square miles, directly adjoining the Waterton Lakes Park of Canada. The Act sounded a caution for the "preservation of the park in a state of nature, so far as consistent with the purpose of the Act," and "for the care and protection of the fish and game" within the park. Unfortunately, there were a great many private holdings within the boundaries. Many difficulties have attended the efforts to clear the park of private property, and the end is not yet.

Rocky Mountain National Park was established in 1915. The park came in with the usual wording that it should be set aside "for the benefit and enjoyment of the people of the United States," but most unfortunately it also provided "that the United States Reclamation Service may enter upon and utilize for flowage or other purposes any area within said park which may be necessary for the development and maintenance of a Government Reclamation project." This provision, as will be seen later, has risen to confound the park administrators, and to curtail the enjoyment of the people in the national park which they have dedicated to the pleasure of the people.

In August of 1916 Kilauea and Haleakala Volcanoes, with protective rims, on the Islands of Hawaii and Maui, were constituted Hawaii National Park by Act of Congress and it was provided that perpetual easements and rights-of-way should be acquired and transferred to the United States.

DR. McFARLAND AND THE NATIONAL PARK SYSTEM

In August of the same year, Lassen Volcanic National Park was created by Congress to protect Lassen Volcano in northern California. As Lassen has been active in recent years, this area has provided a laboratory of research, but the park is also much visited by those who love to camp and fish and so provides a by-product of interesting outdoor life.

Following the Conservation Congress of 1908, Dr. McFarland inaugurated a campaign of education to place the national parks in the hands of a single Federal administrator. In 1910, at his behest, Secretary Ballinger recommended such a bureau in his Annual Report. He stated, "The volume and importance of the work of the supervision of the national parks and reserves under the Secretary of the Interior has passed beyond the stage of satisfactory control by operations carried on with the small force available in the Secretary's office."

At the 1911 Annual Convention of the American Civic Association, President Taft, Secretary of the Interior Fisher, and Dr. McFarland made notable addresses. President Taft made the situation clear when he said: "Now we have in the United States a great many natural wonders, and in that lazy way we have in our Government of first taking up one thing and then another, we have set aside a number of National Parks, of forest reservations covering what ought to be National Parks, and what are called 'national monuments.' We have said to ourselves, 'Those cannot get away. We have surrounded them by a law which makes them necessarily Government property forever, and we will wait in our own good time to make them useful as parks to the people of this country. Since the Interior Department is the "lumber room" of the Government, into which we put everything that we don't know how to classify, and don't know what to do with, we will just put them under the Secretary of the Interior.' That is the condition of the National Parks today."

Secretary Fisher told of the first conference on national parks, held in Yellowstone National Park, under the auspices of the Department of the Interior, with Dr. McFarland as an honored guest and participant. Concerning the proposed Federal agency, he said: "I have talked this matter over with the President, and I know that he is favorably interested in it, and that he gladly accepted the suggestion that he come over here this evening to meet this audience and express his own views in favor of this movement in which the American Civic Association is taking so prominent and leading a part."

Dr. McFarland made a plea, first for the national parks themselves. Said he: "The national playgrounds . . . can, if they are held inviolable, preserve for us, as no minor possessions can, our unique scenic wonders, our great natural mysteries. The spouting geyser basins and marvelous hot springs of the Yellowstone, the atmospheric splendors of the Grand Canyon of the Colorado, the silver threads of the Falls of the Yosemite, the ancient homes of the cliff-dwellers on the Mesa Verde, the ice marvels of the Montana glaciers, the blue marvel of Crater Lake, the towering temples among the big trees of the Sierra—how long would they last unharmed and free to all the people if the hand of the Federal Government were withdrawn from them?"

Speaking of the need for a Federal bureau, Dr. McFarland declared: "Nowhere in official Washington can an inquirer find an office of the National Parks, or a desk devoted solely to their management. By passing around through three departments, and consulting clerks who have taken on the extra work of doing what they can for the Nation's playgrounds, it is possible to come at a little information.

"This is no one's fault. Uncle Sam has simply not waked up about his precious parks. He has not thrown over them the mantle of any complete legal protection—only the Yellowstone has any adequate legal status, and the Yosemite is technically a forest reserve. Selfish and greedy assaults have been made upon the parks, and it is under a legal 'joker' that San Francisco is now seeking to take to herself without having in ten years shown any adequate engineering reason for the assault, nearly half of Yosemite. . . . Now there is light and a determination to do as well for the Nation as any little city does for itself. The Great Father of the Nation, who honors us tonight by his presence, has been the unswerving friend of the Nation's scenic possessions."

Following this memorable meeting in Washington, President Taft sent to Congress on February 2, 1912, a special message: "I earnestly recommend the establishment of a Bureau of National Parks. Such legislation is essential to the proper management of those wondrous manifestations of nature, so startling and so beau-

tiful that everyone recognizes the obligations of the Government
to preserve them for the edification and recreation of the people.

"The Yellowstone Park, the Yosemite, the Grand Canyon of
the Colorado, the Glacier National Park and the Mount Rainier
National Park and others furnish appropriate instances. In only
one case have we made anything like adequate preparation for the
use of a park by the public. That case is the Yellowstone National
Park. Every consideration of patriotism and the love of nature
and of beauty and of art requires us to expend money enough to
bring all these natural wonders within easy reach of our people.
The first step in that direction is the establishment of a responsible
bureau, which shall take upon itself the burden of supervising the
parks and of making recommendations as to the best method of
improving their accessibility and usefulness."

The *Outlook*, in its issue of September 30, 1911, commented upon
the Yellowstone National Park Conference and upon the coöperation of the American Civic Association with the Department of
the Interior: "It is in point to note that, at the instance and with
the approval of the American Civic Association, Secretary Fisher's
predecessor, Mr. Ballinger, had offered during the last session of the
Sixtieth Congress a carefully drawn bill creating such a (bureau)."
In the issue of February 3, 1912, the *Outlook* suggested that the new
bureau be called the National Park Service, in conformity with
the custom already established in naming the Forest Service. The
bill considered by the Sixty-second Congress did in fact adopt
that suggestion.

But when the American Civic Association held its 1912 Convention in Baltimore on November 20, the bill had not passed Congress. Again Secretary Fisher spoke. He said: "We did draw up
and present to Congress a bill for the creation of a Bureau of
National Parks, and this Association was one of the chief agencies
that interested itself in pushing that bill. We had the bill considered in committee, and I think the general result was quite
favorable, but our lawmakers—to indulge in a public confidence—
were so engaged in preparing for the presidential election that
they made little progress for us, and today we confront precisely
the same situation; and though I am here to report progress, there
is not very much progress to report. But I ask this Association
to continue to use all the influence in its power to see that some

effective means is provided to improve these conditions, and to apply sound principles of administration to our National Parks System."

On that occasion, too, the Right Honorable James Bryce, British Ambassador to the United States, made a memorable address. Ambassador Bryce displayed an intimate knowledge of the subject and of United States geography. Said he: "You have prodigious and magnificent forests; there are no others comparable for extent and splendor with those you possess. These forests, especially those on the Cascade range and the Sierra Nevada, are being allowed to be cut down ruthlessly by the lumbermen. I do not blame them; timber is wanted and they want to drive their trade, but the process goes on too fast and much of the charm of nature is lost while the interests of the future are forgotten. The same thing is happening in the Appalachian ranges in New England and the Alleghanies southward from Pennsylvania, a superbly beautiful country, where the forests made to be the delight of those who wish to ramble among them and enjoy the primitive charm of hills and woodland glades, have been despoiled. Sometimes the trees have been cut down and the land left bare. Sometimes an inextricable tangle of small boughs and twigs remains, so that when a dry year comes a fire rages among them and the land is so scorched that for many long years no great trees will rise to replace those that were destroyed." He continued: "You fortunately have a great supply of splendid water power. I am far from saying that a great deal of it, perhaps most of it, may not be very properly used for industrial purposes, but I do say that it has been used in some places to the detriment, and even to the ruin, of scenery."

Ambassador Bryce had visited four of the national parks. After praising their unique beauty, he paid tribute "to the taste and judgment with which, as it seemed to me three years ago, the hotels in the Yosemite were being managed. There were no offensive signs, no advertisements of medicines, no other external disfigurements to excite horror, and the inns were all of moderate size and not more than two stories high. I earnestly hope that the administration will always be continued on these lines, with this same regard for landscape beauty."

The summation of the address seems incontrovertible:

"The world seems likely to last a long, long time, and we ought to make provision for the future.

"The population of the world goes on constantly increasing and nowhere increasing so fast as in North America.

"A taste for natural beauty is increasing, and, as we hope, will go on increasing.

"The places of scenic beauty do not increase, but, on the contrary, are in danger of being reduced in number and diminished in quantity, and the danger is always increasing with the accumulation of wealth, owing to the desire of private persons to appropriate these places. There is no better service we can render to the masses of the people than to set about and preserve for them wide spaces of fine scenery for their delight."

By 1913 there was a new Secretary of the Interior, Franklin K. Lane. Soon after he was inducted into office, Dr. McFarland and Richard Watrous, Secretary of the American Civic Association, called upon him. They laid before him the great need for a National Park Service. Secretary Lane, who came from California and knew the national parks of the West, gave his callers most sympathetic attention. In April of 1914 hearings were held on the Raker bill. Adolph C. Miller, Assistant to the Secretary of the Interior, spoke for Mr. Lane. The bill was approved by the Secretaries of Interior and Agriculture. But the bill was not to pass the Sixty-third session of Congress.

In April of 1916, hearings were again held on two pending bills, one introduced by Judge Raker and one by William Kent. Stephen T. Mather had now become one of the principal actors in the national-park scene, and was taking the initiative for the Department of the Interior. In addition to the officials, Dr. McFarland and Mr. Watrous, of the American Civic Association, were the principal citizen witnesses. Dr. McFarland called attention to the fact that he and his associates had believed that there should be in the bill "whenever it might seem wise for Congress to pass it, a statement of what parks are for." "It was," he said, "Mr. Frederick Law Olmsted who framed the sentence . . . which is now a part of Mr. Kent's bill: 'The fundamental object of these aforesaid parks, monuments, and reservations is to conserve the scenery and the natural and historical objects therein and to provide for the enjoyment of said scenery and objects by the public in any manner and by any means that will leave them unimpaired for the enjoyment of future generations.' "

It was at this hearing that Dr. McFarland produced a letter from Chief Forester Henry S. Graves, written in response to Dr. McFarland's letter, stating that he had heard rumors that the Forester was not in sympathy with the development of national parks under a separate and distinctive administration. Colonel Graves stated bluntly: "Most certainly I am in favor of establishing a national park service, with adequate authority to organize and administer effectively the national parks. . . . I have consistently expressed myself in this way in public and in private. A few weeks ago when you were at my office with the draft of a bill providing for a national park service I again expressed myself as favorable to the idea. At the same time I called your special attention to two points. One was to make certain that the officers in the new park service would all be in the classified civil service. The second matter related to the national monuments. The proposed bill transferred the monuments now under the jurisdiction of the Department of Agriculture to the Department of the Interior. I explained to you the difficulties of administration which would arise from this arrangement and suggested a modification of that part of the bill. . . .

"Your second question is whether 'there is proceeding with my knowledge and consent, within the Forest Service, or through its influence without the Forest Service, any opposition to this bill.' My reply is categorically, no."

And so, with the concurrence of the Departments of Interior and Agriculture, and with the support of the American Civic Association, the American Society of Landscape Architects and the American Scenic and Historic Preservation Society of New York, and with the editorial approval of the *Saturday Evening Post*, the *Outlook* and other journals, the Act of August 25, 1916, was adopted by Congress and approved by President Wilson. For eight years Dr. McFarland had worked in season and out of season, to bring about this result. He had interviewed, in turn, Secretaries Ballinger, Fisher, and Lane, had told his story and converted each one of them. It was not, however, until a deficiency appropriation was made available at the next session of Congress that the Service was organized, with Stephen T. Mather as Director.

STEPHEN T. MATHER AND HIS ASSOCIATES

"Dear Steve: If you don't like the way the parks are being run, come down and run them yourself."
—Franklin K. Lane to Stephen T. Mather in 1914, quoted in address of Horace M. Albright before the American Civic Association, printed in American Civic Annual, 1929.

HORACE M. ALBRIGHT, in an address before the American Civic Association, in 1929, after paying tribute to Dr. McFarland as "the one man who eloquently pleaded for preservation of the scenic resources of our country," who at the conferences in Yellowstone and Yosemite "had helped formulate important protective policies," and who "had been the trusted adviser of two Secretaries of the Interior," told the story of Mr. Mather's connection with the National Park Service: "That (1914) autumn, Secretary Lane got some letters of complaint about conditions in the western parks, especially Sequoia. The letters came from a Chicago businessman who had been spending his summers in the western mountains and parks since 1905, when he climbed Mount Rainier with the Sierra Club, and who had been in the University of California with the Secretary some thirty years before.

"The complaints were fair but firm, and there was an insistent demand that park conditions be improved. The complainant was Stephen T. Mather, borax manufacturer and Sierra Club man. Finally, Secretary Lane wrote him substantially as follows: 'Dear Steve: If you don't like the way the parks are being run, come down and run them yourself.' The letter also contained a serious request to visit him in Washington. Mr. Mather came one cold December day in 1914, and after several days' consideration of the offer made by Mr. Lane, accepted the position of Assistant to the Secretary. . . . After appointing him and getting him settled in an office, he said: 'By the way, Steve, I forgot to ask you your politics.' There was not then and never has been any politics in the National Park Service. . . .

"Mr. Mather's enthusiasm, public spirit, and generosity quickly won him friends in every direction, and especially in Congress. The stage was set for action and results. . . . Both Representatives John E. Raker and William Kent of California introduced the National Park Service bills in the House in the Sixty-fourth Congress, and Senator Smoot introduced the measure in the Senate.

[77]

"After an exciting series of hearings and the surmounting of many unexpected delays and difficulties, on August 25, 1916, the Kent Bill became a law, and the National Park Service was created as the ninth bureau of the Department of the Interior."

Honorable Louis C. Cramton, for many years chairman of the appropriations sub-committee in charge of funds for the Interior Department, in a speech delivered on the floor of the House of Representatives, outlined the early days of the Park Service: "When funds became available for actually establishing the National Park Bureau, Mr. Mather was appointed its first director. In the days of struggle before the creation of the bureau, and for many war years afterwards when funds for civilian bureaus were necessarily limited, Mr. Mather gave freely of his personal funds for the benefit of the National Park System.

"By no means the least factor in Mr. Mather's success in coördinating, administering, and developing the National Park System has been his uncanny ability to pick the right man for a particular job; and the loyalty to the cause, as represented by the chief, has caused many a park superintendent and other officer to give up opportunities for larger financial returns to stick to the 'park game,' as they call it. Working under Mr. Mather has been a game in the truest sense of the word.

"I have, in my service of many years on the Committee on Appropriations, come into rather close contact with many branches of the Government service in Washington and in the field, and nowhere have I seen such uniform devotion to the highest ideals of service to the country, such unselfish team-work, such an *esprit de corps* as in the National Park Service as organized and built up under Stephen T. Mather."

Never did a harassed executive inherit a more chaotic situation. Former Secretaries of the Interior, with little financial support from Congress, had called in the Army to patrol and guard Yellowstone. In some of the parks the Army Engineers built the roads; in others, toll roads had been built and were operated for fees. There was no clear line of demarcation between the responsibility of the Interior and War Departments. Secretary Garrison in 1914 had called to Secretary Lane's attention that appropriations charged to the War Department were really expended for the benefit of the Interior Department, and suggested that the time had come to take over the complete handling of the parks. Provision for caring for the public in hotels and lodges in the national parks was through the system of inviting private capital to erect the necessary buildings and operate them as concessions.

In the early years of his service, as Assistant to the Secretary of the Interior and as Director of the National Park Service, Mr. Mather drew around him a remarkable group of men. Horace M. Albright became Mr. Mather's right-hand man in working out the policies which were to guide the newly created National Park Service. In 1919, Mr. Albright succeeded the military officers in command at Yellowstone, becoming the first civilian superintendent in thirty-two years, and Field Assistant to the Director. In 1927, Mr. Albright, in addition to being Superintendent of Yellowstone, was made Assistant Director (field). When Mr. Mather resigned in 1929 because of ill health, Mr. Albright succeeded him as Director, and served five years in that capacity.

When Mr. Albright went to Yellowstone, Arno B. Cammerer, who had been Secretary of the Commission of Fine Arts, became the Assistant Director of the National Park Service. When Mr. Albright was appointed Director, Mr. Cammerer became Associate Director, and when Mr. Albright resigned in 1933, he was succeeded by Mr. Cammerer. Another man who has been continually with the National Park Service almost from the beginning is Arthur E. Demaray, who served successively as Editor, Administrative Assistant, and Assistant Director, and is now Associate Director of the Service.

After twenty-two years, the administration of the National Park Service is still in the hands of those who worked with Mr. Mather, absorbed his ideas and ideals, and who are striving to carry on the work as they believe Mr. Mather would have desired in the face of changing conditions and increasing responsibilities.

Superintendents called early into the Service who became well-known hosts for Uncle Sam in the parks and are still connected with the Service include George B. Dorr of Acadia National Park, Judge Walter Fry and Colonel John R. White of Sequoia National Park, Jesse Nusbaum of Mesa Verde, Edmund B. Rogers of Rocky Mountain and Yellowstone, Major O. A. Tomlinson of Mt. Rainier, M. R. Tillotson of Grand Canyon, J. Ross Eakin of Glacier, Grand Canyon, and Great Smoky Mountains, Thomas J.

Allen who served in various parks and is now a Regional Director, Eivind Scoyen of Zion, Glacier, and Sequoia, Major Thomas Boles of Hawaii and Carlsbad Caverns, Frank Pinkley in charge of the Southwest Monuments, and many others, too numerous to mention, who have dedicated their best efforts toward serving their trustees, the American people, the owners of the national parks. Three superintendents who died in office and who have left indelible marks on the parks they administered and will long be remembered by park visitors, are W. B. Lewis of Yosemite, Roger W. Toll of Mt. Rainier, Rocky Mountain, and Yellowstone, and Colonel C. G. Thomson of Crater Lake and Yosemite. At the time of the tragic death of Roger Toll, the Park Service also lost another member of the staff, a young man who had done much to develop park ideals and strengthen the service to the public, George M. Wright of California.

The phrase "Stephen T. Mather and his Associates" is, therefore, used advisedly, for the National Park Service today is being administered by the men who helped to develop standards and ideals with him and who have dedicated themselves to carrying on the work which Mr. Mather so nobly began.

Along with many complications and troubles, Mr. Mather inherited certain traditions. The act creating Yellowstone National Park carried three general directions: (1) that the area was being set aside "as a public park or pleasuring ground for the benefit and enjoyment of the people," (2) that all timber, mineral deposits, natural curiosities or wonders within the park should be preserved from injury or spoliation and retained in their natural condition, and (3) that provision should be made against the "wanton destruction of fish and game found within the park, and against their capture or destruction for the purposes of merchandise or profit."

After many earnest discussions with the staff of the National Park Service, on May 13, 1918, Secretary Lane wrote a letter to Mr. Mather setting forth for the information of the public an announcement of the policy of the Park Service. This policy, the Secretary stated, was based on three broad principles: "First, that the national parks must be maintained in absolutely unimpaired form for the use of future generations as well as those of our own time; second, that they are set apart for the use, observation, health, and pleasure of the people; and third, that the national interest must dictate all decisions affecting public or private enterprise in the parks." Stated obversely, the Secretary declared: "The commercial use of these reservations except as specially authorized by law, or such as may be incidental to the accommodation and entertainment of visitors, will not be permitted under any circumstances."

Since many of the national parks had been taken from national forests, and others created from the public domain adjoined existing national forests, it was natural that Mr. Lane should have laid down for the parks a policy on uses commonly permitted and encouraged in national forests. Concerning grazing he indicated to the Director of the National Park Service that in all national parks except Yellowstone he might permit grazing of cattle "in isolated regions not frequented by visitors and where no injury to the natural features of the parks may result from such use." But he banned utterly the grazing of sheep in national parks.

Secretary Lane gave specific instructions to the Director that he "should not permit the leasing of park lands for summer homes," and the reason he gave was this: "It is conceivable, and even exceedingly probable, that within a few years under a policy of permitting the establishment of summer homes in national parks, these reservations might become so generally settled as to exclude the public from convenient access to their streams, lakes, and other natural features, and thus destroy the very basis upon which this national playground system is being constructed." Since the building of summer homes is quite a common practice within the national forests, here was a distinct difference of policy in the national parks. Another difference of policy was announced in the prohibition of the cutting of trees except where absolutely necessary for buildings and other improvements for the accommodation of the public and the administration of the parks, and then the trees were to be removed without injury to the forests or disfigurement of the landscape.

The Secretary pointed out that roads, trails, and buildings should be built to harmonize with the landscape; he directed that all improvements should be carried out "in accordance with a preconceived plan developed with special reference to the preservation of the landscape," and that comprehensive plans for the future development of the national parks should be prepared.

[81]

The many private holdings in the parks, so long to harass the Service, were recognized as a menace to the public character of the parks, and a determination to eliminate them as rapidly as possible was recorded. Automobiles and motorcycles, newer then than now, were to be permitted in all of the national parks, but "mountain climbing, horseback riding, walking, . . . swimming, boating and fishing" were commended along with motoring.

The Secretary encouraged the educational use of the national parks, suggesting special facilities for classes in science and the establishment of museums in the parks.

For the future, the Secretary directed that, in studying new park projects, the Director should seek to find "Scenery of supreme and distinctive quality or some natural feature so extraordinary or unique as to be of national interest and importance."

It may be said in comment that as time has gone on, the tendency has been to stiffen rather than to relax these principles and standards of practice. Hunting never has been permitted in the national parks. Fishing for pleasure is encouraged. Grazing has been eliminated in many places and it is the hope of those now responsible for the administration of the parks that the time may come when there will be no grazing of cattle, as there is now no grazing of sheep in any national park or monument. Except in the rare instances when Congress has directed the introduction of extraneous and undesirable intrusions, and for the non-conforming uses which have sometimes been permitted for a period of years, the national parks have been protected from uses not compatible with their primary purpose. That is why they offer to the public today unrivaled opportunities to see the most beautiful and the most interesting regions in the United States and its possessions.

When Mr. Mather took over the directorship of the national parks, there were seventeen national parks and twenty-one national monuments. Except for the Sieur de Monts National Monument, now Acadia National Park, in Maine, all of the parks and monuments lay west of the Mississippi River. The system then included the national park in Alaska and the two volcanoes in Hawaii.

It will be recalled that the year in which the National Park Service was authorized by Congress saw also the first of the large Federal-aid grants to the States for the building of public highways, and that the month in which the Service was actually organized saw also the entrance of the United States into the World War. These two events exercised a very real influence on the national parks. The war caused an almost complete cessation in pleasure travel, to the extent that it was necessary to make repeated announcements that the national parks were open, as usual, to the public. But perhaps the movement which was to provide hard-surfaced highways for this country has left a more lasting and deeper impression on the parks. Motor travel, at first small in most of the national parks, with the improvement of highways has increased enormously, so that now, in most parks, it exceeds the substantial volume of visitors who come by rail and use buses in the parks. Those who come by rail generally are on "all-expense tours" and stay in the hotels or lodges. Those who come by automobile may patronize the hotels or lodges, but they frequently stay in the cabins or set up their Lares and Penates in the public camps provided for their comfort and convenience.

By some the great increase in visitors to the national parks is deplored. This is a valid criticism, no doubt, in those parks where the crowds are so great that they do actual damage to the park itself and limit the enjoyment of visitors. But it should be realized that the national parks do belong to the American people as a whole, and are open for their enjoyment and edification. When a pitcher of water is full, it will hold no more, and it is now recognized that there is such a thing as a park or a valley *full* of people, and that places of overflow must be provided. In Yosemite Valley, where the greatest congestion is reported, the high Sierra country around the park and the groves of Big Trees have been provided with facilities for caring for guests; these have good roads and trails, so that there is at least the invitation for valley visitors to go into other parts of the park. Probably other methods will need to be used to bring about a dispersal of large crowds at congested centers in the parks.

In Secretary Lane's letter of 1918, there was a direction to the effect that the buildings and other facilities for accommodating visitors be confined to as small an area as feasible. This principle has been followed in providing new facilities in old parks and in planning new parks. Hand in hand with this policy has been the definite aim of the National Park Service to hold great regions in each of the larger parks in as near a natural condition as possible, so that visitors on foot and on horseback might enjoy the wilderness features. It is now clear that if there is to be anything like an adequate supply of wilderness regions in the national parks, these areas must be increased by incorporating into the National Park System those remaining untouched areas which meet the standards set by Yellowstone, Yosemite, and other superlative national parks. Already the inroads on the wilderness have been so great that there are comparatively few unspoiled areas left, just as Ambassador Bryce predicted in 1912. And as the wilderness has been vanishing, the demand for "back country" into which hikers and horseback riders may go is increasing. The trends are unmistakable.

The wisdom of Secretary Lane, Mr. Mather and his associates is increasingly apparent, as time demonstrates the need for the safeguards they set up. The Department of the Interior and the National Park Service have been obliged to accept from the hands of Congress national parks with undesirable easements and rights in them. Congress has even directed the desecration of certain national parks, as in the case of the Hetch Hetchy; but the Department and the Service have striven steadily to decrease and eliminate all adverse uses and practices in the national parks, and to foster restoration to natural conditions wherever possible. It has been found that in meadows which have been grazed for years, the wild flowers will come back in areas protected from grazing.

When Mr. Mather assumed office, there was little understanding of the national parks as a well-defined type of land-use. The public knew about Yellowstone as a land of wonders, and Yosemite as a valley incomparable, but few dreamed that the foundation was being laid for a new and entrancing type of reservation which would bring to young and old much enjoyment and many cultural opportunities.

Mr. Mather put himself and his private fortune at the service of the national parks. He purchased the Tioga Road entrance into Yosemite when he could not secure public appropriations to buy it. He interested his friends in aiding the parks. He lectured on national parks in all parts of the country, and gave to his audiences a new conception of national parks and their service to the public. He explained the difference between national parks and national forests. Even today there is much confused thinking about national parks and national forests.

Definitions sometimes seem tedious, but perhaps it is just as well to present a simple description of each which has been used by the American Civic Association as a measuring rod. According to the Park Primer, issued in four editions, beginning in 1922, "A NATIONAL PARK is an area, usually of some magnitude, distinguished by scenic, scientific, historic, or archeologic attractions and natural wonders and beauties which are distinctly *national* in importance and interest, selected as eminent examples of scenic, scientific or historic America, and preserved with characteristic natural scenery, wildlife and historic or archeologic heritage, in an unimpaired state, as a part of a National Park System for the use and enjoyment of this and future generations."

In this same Park Primer it is recognized that "Recreational uses of the National Forests are valuable to the public and may be broadly and beneficently extended and encouraged, always, however, in the knowledge that the primary purposes of national forests are the provision of timber and the conservation of water-sources, and that dependence for recreational uses of such areas must not lose sight of these primary purposes and other secondary commercial uses of National Forests. In National Forests, grazing and other commercial uses are permitted, hunting and fishing under state laws are allowed, private individuals may erect and occupy summer cottages. There are many beautiful and inspiring views in the National Forests. Especially fine stands of trees are frequently given protection. Forest cover along streams is sometimes left uncut. Study areas of characteristic timber are being set aside to be kept in their primitive state. Many wildlife sanctuaries are contained within National Forests. Generally speaking, the U. S. Forest Service pursues a policy of providing for selective cutting of timber as it becomes ripe for market, as authorized by law; supervises the grazing of herds owned by private individuals, permits fencing of pasture, and meets the economic demands made upon the forests."

Since this was written, the Forest Service has set aside a large number of Primitive Areas by Executive Order of the Secretary of Agriculture. These are generally roadless, but grazing and cutting of timber are not necessarily entirely excluded. The Forest Service is now developing recreation plans for certain areas in which conflicting commercial uses are being excluded or reduced. It so happens that some of the Primitive and Recreation Areas meet all of the national-park standards. These areas were in the forests when they were transferred, often by Executive Order of the President, from the public domain, long before there was a National Park Service. Now that the national-park land-use is recognized, the areas which meet all the national-park standards will undoubtedly, in the course of the next few years, be transferred to the National Park System.

The national parks and monuments have been added to the system carefully. Probably no Federal agency ever existed which has reported adversely on as many proposals for additional lands as has the National Park Service. When the public first became aware of the drawing power of national parks, every community, every State, and every promotion organization wanted to create a national park in its vicinity. One of the most famous fights to keep an area out of the National Park System was made when it was proposed that the Ouachita National Forest be transferred to the National Park Service. It was easily demonstrated that the Ouachita National Forest was being administered under a policy fully adapted to its best possibilities. It was an economic asset in a State which very much needed economic assets. Its scenery, while pleasant, was not outstanding and, in the opinion of land-planning students, would never have drawn a national patronage. Congress refused to consider a change of status, and the Forest Service was permitted to continue its already well-established policy of making the land pay its way.

If the Federal Government were the only agency dealing in parks it might not be possible to apply so strict an entrance examination; but, fortunately, the States are now building creditable State Park Systems to preserve in their natural condition the best examples of State scenery and to provide recreational and educational opportunities for the people of the State. There are also the county and regional parks and parkways in addition to the town and municipal park systems. It is, therefore, possible and practicable to limit national parks to national service.

For the most part, national parks have been added one by one. Mt. McKinley, Alaska, was created in 1917. At the time that the National Park Service was created, Grand Canyon was a national monument administered by the Forest Service. In 1919 it was made a national park by Congress. In the same year Acadia National Park was created to include a national monument and additional land purchased and given to the Government. This same year, Zion, that colorful canyon in Utah, became a national park, and in 1928, Bryce Canyon, which had been a national monument, was transformed into a national park.

Up to this time there had been only one national park in the East, where the public lands had long since passed into private ownership, and yet, almost miraculously there were some areas comparatively free from the scars of civilization. In the twenties, therefore, Secretary Work set up the Southern Appalachian National Park Commission, consisting of Representative Henry W. Temple of Pennsylvania, William C. Gregg of New Jersey, Major William A. Welch of New York, Harlan P. Kelsey then of Massachusetts, but formerly of North Carolina, and Colonel Glenn S. Smith of the Department of the Interior. The Commission was charged with the duty of recommending a national park in the Southern Appalachians. After careful survey of the ground, the Committee reported, recommending the Great Smoky Mountains and a long strip of the Blue Ridge in Virginia. The resulting Temple-Swanson Act authorized the Secretary of the Interior to accept lands for these parks and for Mammoth Cave National Park, in Kentucky. The problem was how to bring these areas, mostly privately owned, back into public ownership. The States of Tennessee and North Carolina appropriated money and raised private subscriptions to purchase the land, but when it seemed that the project was about to fail, Mr. John D. Rockefeller, Jr., made five million dollars available. The Great Smoky Mountains National Park was established for protection in 1930. Mr. Rockefeller helped to the extent of half a million dollars in the purchase of the Blue Ridge area, and the Shenandoah National Park was established in 1935. The Grand Tetons came into the system in 1929. In 1931 Isle Royale in Lake Superior, in 1934 the Everglades in Florida, and in 1935 Big Bend in Texas were authorized. But purchase of the necessary lands has dragged. The areas are not yet national parks.

In the Report of Director Albright, dated October 12, 1932, it was stated that the National Park Service administered twenty-two national parks, totaling some 13,000 square miles, and thirty-six national monuments, totaling some 6,500 square miles. Then on July 28, 1933, President Franklin D. Roosevelt by Executive Order transferred a long list of monuments to the Park Service. This brought under a single central jurisdiction all of the monuments created by Executive Order under the National Antiquities Act, and other miscellaneous areas, some of which have been re-transferred.

Today the National Park Service administers twenty-seven national parks and seventy-three national monuments, covering some seventeen and a half million acres of land and water, of which nearly six million acres lie in Alaska.

It must not be supposed that the national parks, even as they are today, have been easily defended against selfish and unwarranted encroachments. The Hetch Hetchy fight which resulted in turning the Hetch Hetchy yosemite without recompense over to the City and County of San Francisco was one of the most tragic and disastrous experiences in all national-park history. The people of San Francisco did, indeed, invest a vast sum of money in the making of the reservoir and in construction of the necessary accompanying works—something like a hundred million dollars, it is reported; but many engineers now think that a much smaller expenditure would have brought to the city all that was needed. There never was any claim that there were not alternative physical schemes, only that this proposal could be carried out more cheaply. And now even this claim seems disproved. It may take hundreds of years, but perhaps some day this great continent will be inhabited by a race of people who value their heritage of natural scenery so highly that they will redeem the Hetch Hetchy, and allow Nature to go to work with her age-taking remedies to restore the beauty that has been unthinkingly given away!

The Grand Canyon National Park, one of the most marvelous spectacles in the entire world, has been subject to repeated attacks. Its first protection came when, aroused by a reported project to encircle the rim by a sight-seeing electric trolley line, Gifford Pinchot, stirred up by Dr. McFarland, persuaded "Teddy" Roosevelt to make it a national monument by Executive Order. Thirty-two years were required to establish it as a national park, and when Congress did act in 1919, mining and grazing were permitted under the act. Since then, the mining provision has been revoked, but not until after a long fight, in which mining claims, outrageously enough, were staked along the Bright Angel Trail in a way to give a monopoly to the holders to conduct trips along this trail from the rim into the floor of the canyon far below! At last it was proved that these claims were not filed or maintained in good faith. The park is now safe from new filings, and old claims have been abrogated.

By Act of Congress in 1891, the Secretary of the Interior was authorized to grant, under certain conditions, rights-of-way in Yosemite, Sequoia, and General Grant parks for the construction of electrical plants and all their paraphernalia—reservoirs, mining, quarrying, and cutting of timber. In 1911 this authority was slightly amended to limit easements to fifty years, and in 1921 such installations were made by law subject to specific action of Congress.

Another menacing threat to three national parks was included in the acts of dedication—all before the creation of the National Park Service. In Glacier, Rocky Mountain, and Lassen National Parks, there was an identical provision that "the U. S. Reclamation Service may enter upon and utilize for flowage or other purposes any area within said park which may be necessary for the development and maintenance of a Government reclamation project." In the Grand Canyon Act, passed in 1919, the wording varies slightly, but does permit reclamation projects.

It just happened that at the time these parks were created, this country had been stirred by the new possibilities opened up through the reclamation of arid lands in the West. There were not only great engineers who installed the systems, but there were minor prophets who heralded reclamation as a deliverance which would give happy homes and pleasant living to many independent farmers. No one at that date knew, or apparently cared, whether the projects were economically sound, and certainly there were few who foresaw the era of over-production and stabilized population into which we were heading.

Perhaps it was not unnatural, therefore, that Secretary Lane, in whose Department the Reclamation Service was an established bureau, who was himself an ardent believer in the rosy promise of reclamation for the West, and who had only recently been introduced to his responsibilities concerning national parks, should not at once have realized that reclamation was incompatible with national parks. Indeed, Robert B. Marshall, whose training had been as a geographer, during the time when he was serving as Superintendent of National Parks, prior to the appointment of

Mr. Mather as Director, consistently advised the Secretary to look out for the interests of reclamation in all pending measures to create new national parks.

It was not until Judge John Barton Payne became Secretary of the Interior in 1920 that the National Park Service found a complete advocate. With his keen brain and his training in legal practice and on the bench, Judge Payne at once saw that if national parks were to survive at all, they must be held inviolate from adverse uses. In recent years public opinion has come to support the platform laid down by Judge Payne. Succeeding Secretaries of the Interior have generally supported the policies of the Park Service. Secretaries Wilbur and Ickes came in as known conservationists. In 1931 Congress wiped out many special privileges. In Rainier, Glacier, and Rocky Mountain parks authority for railway franchises was repealed; in Mesa Verde and Grand Canyon authorization for prospecting was abrogated; in Mt. McKinley prospecting was sharply restricted.

The one national park which came to us without strings of any kind is the first—Yellowstone. And yet predatory interests in Montana and Idaho have tried again and again to set up profitable enterprises in this park—profitable, it may be explained, because of the *free* storage they hoped to secure on the top of Yellowstone Lake, or from free franchises for railroads. From 1884 to 1893, private interests sought unsuccessfully to secure from Congress the authority for a right-of-way for a railroad through Yellowstone National Park, and when the proposal met resistance, an effort was made to eliminate the desired lands from the park. Louis Cramton, a member of Congress for eighteen years, in his "Early History of Yellowstone National Park and Its Relation to National Park Policies," issued in 1932, told of the years in which the House of Representatives seemed "amenable to the desire of these private interests, and the Senate was the stronghold of opposition under the leadership of Senator Vest, but," declared Mr. Cramton, "finally the time came that any railroad right-of-way proposal or park segregation scheme brought definite adverse report from Congressional committees."

One of the great menaces to national parks came with the passage of the Federal Water Power Act of 1920, which would have opened all national parks to power installations. Secretary Payne opposed the signing of the measure by President Wilson.) It was only when a "gentleman's agreement" was reached between the leaders in Congress and the President that at the next session they would give active support to an amendment which would exclude national parks from the provisions of the act, that President Wilson finally signed the measure. (In the next session of Congress, it appeared that, though the Congressional leaders were not disposed to recede from their promise, they personally would not have been disappointed if their efforts had met with failure. In other words, they apparently did not feel that they had guaranteed success. Dr. McFarland, representing the American Civic Association, was active, in coöperation with other conservation organizations, in making it impossible for the proposed amendment to fail. Finally the amendment was passed in the closing days of the session and all existing national parks were definitely excluded from the provisions of the Federal Water Power Act

In the meantime, both Montana and Idaho were pushing their claims for the waters of Lake Yellowstone. Montana desired a dam at the outlet of the lake, which lies high on the crest of the Rocky Mountains, in order to control the flow of flood waters into Montana. At the hearings there was ample testimony to the effect that the proposal, which was advanced by politicians to win political favor, was not even a sound engineering enterprise. Fortunately, Judge Payne made it clear at this hearing that Yellowstone Lake should not be tampered with. He saw clearly that such a commercial invasion in the hitherto inviolate Yellowstone Park would not only grievously injure the park but would ultimately set a precedent which would wreck other parks. In Judge Payne, the proposers of commercial works in national parks met their Waterloo.

At the same time that these Montana proposals were pending in the early twenties, Idaho proposed to build a reservoir in the southwest corner of Yellowstone, and finally, when it appeared that Congress was unwilling to grant such permission, a movement was set on foot to remove the area bodily from the park. This measure was fought bitterly by the National Park Service and the conservation organizations. Idaho at that time also proposed to divert water from Lake Yellowstone through a tunnel across the Divide. This proposal was revived in the last Congress and will undoubtedly appear again, though it does not seem probable that Congress will depart from the policy of nearly sixty years which has given Yellowstone National Park absolute protection from commercial projects.

The action of Congress in authorizing the Colorado-Big Thompson water diversion project was fought by all the conservation organizations, insofar as it affected Rocky Mountain National Park. Unfortunately, the provision in the act creating the park was still in effect. Moreover, the Reclamation Service made definite representations that there would be no need to enter on the park land in the construction of the tunnel underneath. The damage would fall principally on Grand Lake, the rim of which had already suffered from private occupation, and upon the Big Thompson approach highway. The time will come when national park approach roads will receive legal protection, but at the present time these roads are under various state and local jurisdictions. When they pass through national forests they have received some protection, and the tendency is to exercise increased care in nearby cutting operations.

Perhaps this account of the service which Mr. Mather and his associates have rendered to the American people in giving responsible custodianship to lands hitherto open to many misuses, in their efforts to free the parks from legal handicaps and threatened invasions, and in developing and adopting standards for qualifications and uses of the national parks, can best be closed by presenting a "Who's Who" in the National Park Service of today:

Arno B. Cammerer, Director; Arthur E. Demaray, Associate Director; John R. White, Acting Chief of Operations; George A. Moskey, Chief Counsel; Carl P. Russell, Supervisor of Research and Information; Conrad L. Wirth, Supervisor of Recreation and Land Planning; Ronald F. Lee, Supervisor of Historic Sites; Oliver G. Taylor, Chief of Engineering; Thomas C. Vint, Chief of Planning; John D. Coffman, Chief of Forestry; Isabelle F. Story, Editor-in-Chief; Miner R. Tillotson, Director, Region I, Richmond, Virginia; Thomas J. Allen, Jr., Director, Region II, Omaha, Nebraska; Hillory A. Tolson, Acting Director, Region III, Santa Fé, New Mexico; and Frank A. Kittredge, Director, Region IV, San Francisco, California.

Book II—Journeys

PROSPECT: PHILOSOPHY OF PARKS AND PEOPLE

MAN, himself a product of Nature, has in the years since he emerged into the species *Homo sapiens*, spent considerable time—eons, in fact—in creating a man-made environment. This is superimposed upon or takes the place of Nature's Garden of Eden. In the process, Man has destroyed, or marred beyond recognition, much beautiful landscape. Thus, today a great part of the civilized world lives in the close ranks of city dwellings, surrounded by concrete-covered ground, in buildings of brick, stone, and steel which more or less effectively cut off the free sun and air provided by Nature. These human beings are often completely divorced from contact with the Earth. Indeed, today, were it not for city and regional parks and playgrounds, many children would not know at first hand anything about the trees, the streams, and the growing plant life which played such an important part, economically and emotionally, in the lives of the pioneers in America. The park zoo for many millions is the only place where children and adults actually see animals other than domestic cats and dogs or caged birds.

But, it may be said, the civilization which produced cities and city life has brought with it refinements of living and culture in art, music, literature, and learning unknown to aboriginal man. Without deprecating what the Arts and Sciences have done to lift Man from primitive living conditions (in which danger to life and limb no doubt counterbalanced the healthful advantages of living in the open) and to enlarge his opportunities for acquiring "knowledge of information," it is pertinent to inquire whether his narrowed contact with Nature has taken away from Man something of value which it is desirable to recapture.

Perhaps the false sense of importance which comes to many large money-makers in the marts of trade, to successful politicians, to the producers of lucrative jazz in art and music, and to all who gain power not based on human service, is one of the regrettable losses visited upon Man by man-made civilization. The great men of the past—teachers, scientists, statesmen, artists, musical composers, creators of living literature—have nearly always possessed a quality of humility. They studied the history of men, institutions, and ideas which transcends the history of single individuals. Or they studied Science, which yields knowledge reluctantly, bit by bit, as a reward for persistent search and questioning, and invariably leaves the student with the realization that there is a vast reservoir of knowledge and laws which limited intelligence and mental powers have yet failed to penetrate. Or they listened to an inner voice or followed an inner light, and so came to be called inspired. These "great" discovered in various ways some inkling of the laws of life and living beyond their making. Their humility came from a realization that they were but an infinitesimal part of a Universe so great that it beggars human comprehension. They learned that they were subject to laws which, however little understood, moved inexorably; that, without choice, they came into the world and faced or sought to escape its problems.

Primitive peoples read the laws of Nature dimly, perhaps, and personified in their gods and superstitions the little knowledge that they sensed. But the "gods" kept them disciplined and humble. Today, many of the peoples who have cast off the formalized religions and superstitions of the past have also lost contact with the manifestations of Nature and the laws of the Universe. They have lost their sense of proportion, and their perspective has become distorted.

Moreover, the city habits of living indoors and of intense application to mundane problems, wear men out before their time. At best, the span of human life is short. Consider how many businessmen, who now live in an age when Science has contributed to the lengthening of human life, find themselves at fifty or sixty with wrecked digestions, worn-out hearts, hardened arteries or victims of some of the hundred-and-one diseases due to slothful indoor physical habits and continuous mental strain. It is a paradox that, with the possible prolongation of life, there are so many who cannot enjoy the later years saved to them by Science.

John Muir, who became in his middle years a successful orchardist, always referred to his earlier years in the Sierra, when he earned little money, ate sparingly, and wandered much, as the "free" years of his life. He might have called them the "rich" years of his life, when he was not encumbered with possessions and their care. This is no argument for avoiding responsibility or for escaping duties. But it is an argument for the rejuvenation and the restoration of equilibrium which comes from outdoor recreation.

One of the proverbial joys of youth comes from pleasure in physical movement and muscular well-being. Outdoor recreation can continue to give equal pleasure to the middle-aged and elderly, if they are able to ward off the painful diseases which attack the muscles and nerves of over-fed and under-exercised bodies.

But far beyond the pleasure of walking or riding horseback in the ordinary open country, indulging the eyes in pleasant prospects, feeling the welcome warmth of the sun and the revivifying breezes of the air, is the spiritual uplift which comes from the contemplation of superlative scenery. Man is indeed "in tune with the Infinite" when he scales high mountains and looks upon stupendous scenes.

Conrad Gesner, writing in 1555, as quoted in translation in the *Sierra Club Bulletin* of April, 1938, expressed something of this exaltation when he said: "For how great the pleasure, how great think you, are the joys of the spirit, touched as is fit it should be, in wondering at the mighty mass of mountains while gazing upon their immensity and, as it were, in lifting one's head among the clouds. In some way or other the mind is overturned by their dizzying height and is caught up in contemplation of the Supreme Architect."

Writing in the present period, Professor G. M. Trevelyan has not only traced the influence of natural beauty on human beings but has declared that sensitivity to fine scenery is indeed an index of the plane on which men and women are living. His words carry conviction: "The appeal of natural beauty is more commonly or at least more consciously felt today than ever before, just because it is no new argument, no new dogma, no doctrine, no change of fashion, but something far older yet far more fresh, fresh as when the shepherd on the plains of Shinar first noted the stern beauty of the patient stars. Through the loveliness of nature, through the touch of sun or rain, or the sight of the shining restlessness, we feel 'Unworded things and old to our pained heart appeal.' And to the young who have no pain, who have not yet kept watch on man's mortality, nature is a joy responding to their own, haunting them like a passion.

"This flag of beauty, hung out by the mysterious Universe, to

[95]

claim the worship of the heart of man—what is it, and what does its signal mean to us? There is no clear interpretation. But that does not lessen its value. Like the Universe, like Life, natural beauty also is a mystery. But whatever it may be, whether casual in its origin as some hold who love it well, or whether as others hold, such splendor can be nothing less than the purposeful message of God—whatever its interpretation may be, natural beauty is the ultimate spiritual appeal of the Universe, of Nature, or of the God of Nature, to their nursling, man. It and it alone makes a common appeal to the sectaries of all our religious and scientific creeds, to the lovers of all our different schools of poetry and art, ancient and modern, and to many more beside these. It is the highest common denominator in the spiritual life of today."

Scenery breaks down into countless appeals—the air itself, the clouds, the mountain masses having form, texture, and color; water, restless and seething or smooth and quiet; all the plant cover from the tiny little ferns and fungi to the Big Trees. It is even inseparably linked to the birds and the beasts, large and small, living in their native habitats.

John Muir, in his Journal of 1868, spoke of the air. A young man on adventure bent, he was tramping down the Santa Clara Valley: "It was now springtime and the weather was the best we ever enjoyed. Larks and streams sang everywhere; the sky was cloudless, and the whole valley was a lake of light. The atmosphere was spicy and exhilarating. . . . This San José sky was not simply pure and bright, and mixed with plenty of well-tempered sunshine, but it possessed a positive flavor, a *taste* that thrilled throughout every tissue of the body. Every inspiration yielded a well-defined piece of pleasure that awakened thousands of new palates everywhere. Both my companion and myself had lived on common air for nearly thirty years, and never before this discovered that our bodies contained such multitudes of palates, or that this mortal flesh, so little valued by philosophers and teachers, was possessed of so vast a capacity for happiness.

"We were new creatures, born again, and truly not until this time were we fairly conscious that we were born at all. Never more, thought I as we strode forward at faster speed, never more shall I sentimentalize about getting free from the flesh, for it is steeped like a sponge in immortal pleasure."

[96]

PROSPECT: PHILOSOPHY OF PARKS AND PEOPLE

John C. Van Dyke, writing thirty-three years later, in 1901, commented on the air of the New World. Said he: "We have often heard of sunny Italy or the 'clear light' of Egypt, but believe me there is no sunlight there compared with that which falls upon the upper peaks of the Sierra Madre or the uninhabitable wastes of the Colorado Desert. Pure sunlight requires for its existence pure air, and the Old World has little of it left. . . . The same thick air is all over Europe, all around the Mediterranean, even over in Mesopotamia and by the banks of the Ganges. It has been breathed and burned and battle-smoked for ten thousand years. Ride up and over the high table lands of Montana—and one can still ride for days without seeing a trace of humanity—and how clear and scentless, how absolutely intangible that sky-blown sun-shot atmosphere! You breathe it without feeling it, you see through it a hundred miles and the picture is not blurred by it."

This ethereal air, then, is one of the first characteristics of national parks—one that is rapidly destroyed when, in the dry season, too many human beings are introduced into spaces which lose their clear air as they are too densely occupied.

Both John Muir and John Van Dyke deplored the damage to the wilderness character of the beautiful places of the earth. In 1897 Muir wrote: "The axe and saw are insanely busy, chips are flying thick as snowflakes, and every summer thousands of acres of priceless forests, with their underbrush, soil, springs, climate, and religion, are vanishing away in clouds of smoke."

Four years later, Van Dyke wrote: "With the coming of civilization the grasses and the wild flowers perish, the forest falls and its place is taken by brambles, the mountains are blasted in the search for minerals, the plains are broken by the plow and the soil is gradually washed into the rivers. Last of all, when the forests have gone the rains cease falling, the streams dry up, the ground parches and yields no life, and the artificial desert—the desert made by the tramp of human feet—begins to show itself. Yes; everyone must have cast a backward glance and seen Nature's beauties beaten to ashes under the successive marches of civilization."

Perhaps we must condone, or at least accept as inevitable, a certain amount of destruction and spoliation through the occupation of the land by the increasing horde of human beings, though it does seem strange that, as Van Dyke remarked: "Today, after

centuries of association, every bird and beast and creeping thing
—the wolf in the forest, the antelope on the plain, and wild fowl
in the sedge—fly from his (man's) approach. They know his
civilization means their destruction. Even the grizzly, secure in
the chaparral of his mountain home, flinches as he crosses the
white man's trail. The boot mark in the dust smells of blood and
iron. The great annihilator has come, and fear travels with him.''

And where Man and his buildings, his roads and his great waste
piles do not penetrate, where even the sawmills have spared the
trees, the cattle and sheep have spread over the forest undergrowth
and in the mountain meadows and swept away from the surface
of the earth the beauty and safety of the covering blanket furnished
by Nature. Muir, in "My First Summer in the Sierra," following
his flock, told of the high Yosemite country near Crane Flat:
"We passed a number of charming garden-like meadows lying on
top of the divide or hanging like ribbons down its sides, imbedded
in the glorious forest. Some are taken up chiefly with . . . a
robust, hearty, liliaceous plant, fond of water and determined to
be seen. Columbine and larkspur grow on the dryer edges of the
meadows, with a tall handsome lupine standing waist-deep in long
grasses and sedges. Castilleias, too, of several species make a bright
show with beds of violets at their feet. But the glory of these
forest meadows is a lily. . . . The tallest are from seven to eight
feet high with magnificent racemes of ten to twenty or more small
orange-colored flowers; they stand out free in open ground, with
just enough grass and other companion plants about them to fringe
their feet, and show them off to best advantage. This . . . lily
. . . is a true mountaineer, reaching prime vigor and beauty at
a height of seven thousand feet. . . . And to think that the sheep
should be allowed in these lily meadows! after how many centuries
of Nature's care planting and watering them, tucking the bulbs
in snugly below winter frost, shading the tender roots with clouds
drawn above them like curtains, pouring refreshing rain, making
them perfect in beauty, and keeping them safe by a thousand
miracles; yet, strange to say, allowing the trampling of devastating
sheep. One might reasonably look for a wall of fire to fence such
gardens. . . . And so the beauty of lilies falls on angels and
men, bears and squirrels, wolves and sheep, birds and bees, but as
far as I have seen, man alone, and the animals he tames, destroy

these gardens. Awkward, lumbering bears . . . love to wallow in them in hot weather, and deer with their sharp feet cross them again and again, sauntering and feeding, yet never a lily have I seen spoiled by them. Rather, like gardeners, they seem to cultivate them, pressing and dibbling as required. Anyhow not a leaf or petal seems misplaced."

This New World, which came fresh from Nature into our hands less than three hundred years ago, has suffered incredibly from the scars of our occupation. Great forests have gone and left sad cut-over lands, as in Michigan. The grassy plains where the buffalo roamed have become the "dust bowl." All game has been depleted and many species exterminated.

National parks cannot indeed bring to life extinct species, but they can and do offer sanctuary to the wildlife which still exists, and in the national parks the visitor may, if he strays from the motor roads, find friendly game, for the birds and the beasts seem to know when they are protected. In the national parks man need not be feared by the animals. He may have the priceless experience of making friends with the trustful deer and the gentle moose, though perhaps he should not meet the predatory bear too carelessly!

About the only views which cannot be harmed by man are the skies and clouds. John Muir wrote frequently in appreciation of the clouds. Wordsworth in his "Guide,to the Lake District" referred to the "skiey influences" which brought such pleasure.

The emotional and spiritual enjoyment of unspoiled scenery, especially when it is on the "ten-league canvas" scale, may indeed bring a new religion and play an important part in the continuance of our particular civilization, for it is as sure as that Babylon and Nineveh are no more that New York and San Francisco will one day be deserted or eclipsed by a new occupation, unless we are able to command a spiritual stamina not developed by close-pressed humanity devoted solely to trade and material welfare.

Many words have been written in prose and poetry about the forms, colors, lights, and shades of the mountains. Wordsworth cautioned his readers that walks in the early morning ought to be taken on the eastern side of the vales, otherwise they will "lose the morning light, first touching the tops and thence creeping down the sides of the opposite hills, as the sun ascends," but he sagely remarked: "It is upon the *mind* which a traveler brings along with him that his acquisitions, whether of pleasure or profit, must principally depend."

Both Wordsworth and John Muir loved storms. At Muir Inlet, Glacier Bay, Alaska, Muir wrote in June of 1890: "Orchestral harmony of the storm, the wind in fine tune, the whole sky one waterfall. . . . How hazy and trivial all selfish pursuits seem at such times, when the whole brave world is in a rush and roar and ecstasy of motion—air and ice and water and the mighty mountains rejoicing in their strength and singing in harmony! . . . Storms are never counted among the resources of a country, yet how far they go towards making brave people. No rush, no corrupting sloth among people who are called to cope with storms with faces set, whether this ministry of beauty be seen or no. . . . The storm was a grand festival." Nearly twenty years before, in the Yosemite, Muir had written: "The storms of winter which so exalt and glorify mountains strike terror into the souls of those who are unacquainted with them, or who have only seen the lights of cities, but to anyone who is in actual contact with the wilderness, these storms are only emphatic words of Nature's love."

The variety of Nature is infinite. It is only in the monotony of city streets and conventional patterns of living that boredom becomes oppressive.

It may seem that the importance of walking and horseback riding and of actual contact with the Earth is over-emphasized. Certainly the acme of enjoyment involves more than being borne in a smooth-running car and *seeing* color, form, light, and shade, and *hearing* the more obvious sounds of Nature. The liquid notes of water slipping over smooth stones, the roar of the frothing cascades, the rustling of the leaves on the trees, the songs of the undisturbed birds, the calls of the wild animals can be heard only in comparative peace and quiet. Only faintly, if at all, can this finer music be heard by those who ride in automobiles, especially when they are part of a fast-moving procession in the midst of noises and smells from the exhausts of hundreds or thousands of motors. It must be recognized that the full aesthetic and emotional effect of delicate scenic pictures cannot be experienced when in rapid motion. To see the national parks adequately, if one is bound to an automobile, one must frequently stop to make use of the many "lookouts" provided by a thoughtful Government and one must, if one is able to walk on shopping expeditions or on golf links, *walk* on the inviting trails which radiate from every camp, inn, or museum group.

But the automobile is not to be despised. It carries the most ardent of walkers and horseback riders to the portals of the wilderness. It makes it possible for everyone to reach the high places on the face of the earth. Sometimes only a few hundred yards from the highway, one may find lonesome-looking places and may sense in some degree the excitement of standing alone to gaze on far-distant views. But, as one who stands high on a "peak in Darien," it is the lover of Nature who strays from the beaten path and the man-made trails who may reach the most sublime heights of emotional and spiritual climax. These are super experiences, to be treasured and remembered as long as one lives.

It is well known that a knowledge of music, its principles, its themes, its harmonies, and its repertory of fine compositions, adds greatly to the *capacity* to enjoy it. A musically ignorant person may be much moved emotionally by a great piece of music, but an educated listener will be more discriminating and understanding without necessarily sacrificing the elemental emotions set astir by great music.

So it is with the work of Nature. What we are accustomed to call a fine scene is always much more than that. An eye sensitive to beauty might see only the contours and colors which exert in themselves a highly emotional influence on the beholder. But the Scientist has made it possible for even the casual travelers to learn something of the age-old forces which have created the scene. The informed beholder may become discriminatingly appreciative.

In the national parks, the museum exhibits and the nature trails offer incomparable opportunities for visitors to penetrate the mysteries of creation which have been in process for a long, long time. They may make the acquaintance of the mighty glaciers on the ground and see how they have worked and are working. They may become friendly with the flowers and the trees and learn to greet them by name. They may see the birds and the beasts living their accustomed lives. All this and more can be the reward of those who visit the national parks by train or automobile, with only a moderate amount of walking.

In 1928, Secretary of the Interior Ray Lyman Wilbur appointed a Committee on the Study of Educational Problems in the National Parks. On the committee were Harold C. Bryant, Hermon C. Bumpus, Vernon Kellogg, John C. Merriam, and Frank R. Oastler. These scientists stressed the inspirational and educational values existing in national parks and recommended a program of interpretation which would enrich the experience of every park visitor. The result was a stimulation of the park museums, park observation stations, the development of guided trips on nature trails and throughout the parks, the increased use of the auto caravans, the enlivening of the campfire talks and the encouragement of college and school trips into the parks for purposes of study. The large number of tourists who join in all of these activities in the national parks, where there is no compulsory school law, has proved that education of this sort can be made alluring.

All this and more is described in an illustrated seventy-page pamphlet on "Research and Education in the National Parks" by Harold Bryant and Wallace W. Atwood, Jr.

That there is much to learn from cosmic forces cannot be denied. Archibald Rutledge, writing in *American Forests*, told of a summer visit to Virginia Beach, where "either to the northward or to the southward of the resort proper, one may walk for lonely miles the magnificent beach." Here on a starry August night, in the light of a "white-winger moon," with the Atlantic rolling in "indolent power and placid triumph," Mr. Rutledge heard "above the muffled music of the surf," a low humming, and overhead, a thousand feet up, he saw the lights of a mail plane. Then he looked at the forest, the ocean, the moon, and the stars. He saw "Capella dipping below the verge on mighty wings of light; Vega . . . steadfast in her destined place, yet holding a speed no mind could reckon; and where the Known and Unknown dimly merged," he watched "how Aldebaran kept his tremendous course." The comparison of man-made miracles of speed with the infinitely greater speed of the stars in their courses is obvious. Mr. Rutledge was right when he said: "About us everywhere is the hush of mystery, the pregnant silence of the undivulged. Over the land and over the sea, brooding on imperial mountains, gleaming in the shy wildflower's little brimming eyes is this sense of promise, of the coming fulfilment of even more than our dreams. In the natural world we have been lovingly preceded. Nature is tremendous with the music of rhythmic laws, the full discovery of which will serve to emancipate our hearts, making us full masters of our destiny."

Dr. John C. Merriam, in his book on "The Living Past," has given an entrancing account of the discovery of a cave in California which revealed past history far back of anything known to man, and which also proved the accuracy of an Indian legend. Dr. Merriam explained: "Though the story came to us repeatedly, it was always in the same form: of a cave with a magic pool called in the Indian language, 'Samwel,' and that it was visited on account of the potency of its water in bringing good fortune. Always it concluded with an account of three maidens who failed to obtain good luck at the pool, and were told by a very aged woman of other water with stronger magic. A second pool was said to lie in a remote chamber, and to escape discovery excepting for the most adventurous. In the course of a long search for this more powerful charm the three maidens came to a pit with sloping borders. As they approached the entrance, one slipped on the moist rock. The others tried to save her, but she fell screaming into the darkness. They heard her 'strike and strike again, and all was still.' A rescue party was unable to reach the bottom of the well and efforts to find the maiden were abandoned." To prove the story true, the well was discovered, and there was the skeleton of the maiden. Dr. Merriam declared: "The body had not moved from the spot where the girl crashed against the solid stone immediately under the opening. Only the bones and a film of black mould remained. Here and there a beginning crystal of stalagmite gleamed in the dark covering, but the lapse of time had not been great enough to allow the lime deposited from dripping water to form a complete shroud. . . . Scattered about, wherever we looked, were the skulls and parts of skeletons of many animals, some so deeply covered with lime as almost to merge with the floor. The mountain lion at the foot of the ladder was heavily encased and cemented in the rock. Near the skeleton of the maiden was a large skull with gracefully curving horns. No head like it had been known to man before. Close by lay another creature with wide-sweeping, oxlike horns—a type of animal then seen for the first time. Across the cave was the perfect skull of a bear, incrusted and cemented to the floor. No human had known this type alive or dead. Spread before us was a veritable museum of ancient life, including also deer, squirrel, porcupine, raccoon, fox, rabbit, and many others. . . . The remains we saw . . . represented a stage in ancient life of America long antedating the fauna now ranging over mountains and valleys of northern California. . . . The scant traces of original material covering the skeleton of the Indian maiden, and the incomplete lime incrustation upon the bones, indicated that entrance of the girl into the cave had been at a very recent period compared with that of the strange creatures among whose heavily incrusted skeletons she had come to rest."

This miracle book of the past may be a bit unusual. But in the national parks and many other untouched areas in the United States are to be found records of past life which excite the imagination and lift the mists which have enshrouded the long-past ages of life upon this Earth. These signs of comparatively recent human and animal tragedies were read just as John Muir read the signs of the far-more-ancient glaciers carving the walls of Yosemite and other Sierra valleys.

Sigurd Olson, writing in a recent issue of *American Forests*, has made a plea for the wilderness. Drawing on his personal experiences, he has told us: "As a guide in the primitive lake regions of the Hudson's Bay watershed, I have lived with men from every walk of life, have learned to know them more intimately than their closest friends at home, their dreams, their hopes, their aspirations. I have seen them come from the cities down below, worried and sick at heart, and have watched them change under the stimulus of wilderness living into happy, carefree, joyous men, to whom the successful taking of a trout or the running of a rapids meant far more than the rise and fall in stocks and bonds. Ask these men what it is they have found and it would be difficult for them to say. This they do know, that hidden back there in the country beyond the steel and the traffic of towns is something real, something as definite as life itself, that for some reason or other is an answer and a challenge to civilization.

"At first, I accepted the change that was wrought with the matter of factness of any woodsman, but as the years went by I began to marvel at the infallibility of the wilderness formula. I came to see that here was a way of life as necessary and as deeply

OLYMPIC MOUNTAINS:
CLAD IN GREEN LUXURIANT
FORESTS

Photograph—Clive
Courtesy—American Forests

[105]

Photograph—Asahel Curtis   Courtesy—American Fore

DOUGLAS FIR AND HEMLOCK IN THE HOH VALLEY, WHICH EXTENDS DEEP INTO
THE OLYMPICS, AT A LOW ALTITUDE, TO THE NORTH WALL OF MT. OLYMPUS

Photograph—Asahel Curtis

Courtesy—American Forests

SEVEN LAKES BASIN, NEAR THE HEAD OF SOLEDUCK RIVER

OLYMPIC NATIONAL PARK

GLACIER LILIES, OLYMPIC NATIONAL PARK

Photograph—Department of the Interior

Courtesy—Planning and Civic Comment

Photographs—Asahel Curtis MT. SEATTLE ABOVE——MT. OLYMPUS BELOW Courtesy—American Fore

rooted in some men as the love of home and family, a vital cultural aspect of life which brought happiness and lasting content."

Continuing, Mr. Olson has remarked: "It is surprising how quickly a man sheds the habiliments of civilization and how soon he feels at home in the wilds."

The philosophy of the wilderness is one of sturdy self-reliance and not one of dependence, according to Mr. Olson. "Men have found at last that there is a penalty for too much comfort and ease, a penalty of lassitude and inertia and the frustrated feeling that goes with unreality." Mr. Olson would not disturb the peace of those who are content with life as they find it—"the picnickers and the strollers, and for them are highways and gravelled trails and country clubs. For them scenic vistas of the wild from the shelter of broad and cool verandas." But for those who "hunger and thirst" for the wilderness as a means of "escape from the perplexing problems of everyday life and freedom from the tyranny of wires, bells, schedules and pressing responsibilities," there is a reward in "peace of mind and relaxation," and "with this escape comes perspective. Far from the towns and all they denote, engrossed in their return to the old habits of wilderness living, men begin to wonder if the speed and pressure they have left are not a little senseless. . . . I believe that here is a sensation born of perspective that most men know in any wilderness. Whenever it comes, men are conscious of a unity with the primal forces of creation and all life that swiftly annihilates the feeling of futility, frustration and unreality. When men realize that they are on their own, that if they are to be sheltered and fed, and, what is more, returned to civilization, they must depend entirely on their own ingenuity, everything they do assumes a tremendous importance. . . . Life soon develops a new and fascinating angle and days which to the uninitiated may seem humdrum or commonplace are filled with the adventure of living for its own sake."

Mr. Olson realizes that the whole world cannot come back to primitive living, but he advocates for a short time each year that city dwellers repair "not necessarily to the great wildernesses of the Arctic or the Canadian lakes, but to some wild part of the country which has not yet been entirely caught up in some scheme of exploitation or development."

We must realize, with Mr. Olson, that the greater part of the wilderness is gone, but in North America we do yet possess a rich estate in wilderness if we are only wise enough to salvage it.

In the national parks are many "oddities" of Nature, such as are found in Yellowstone, many spectacular scenes, such as the Grand Canyon of the Colorado, which draw to them great crowds of sightseers and which will remain popular until the end of time, but there are also in the national parks great unspoiled areas penetrated only by trail or completely free from the scars of man. These are precious possessions. But they are all too limited. There are many more wilderness areas useful principally for their inspirational and stabilizing effect on mankind, which should be brought into the parks, where they will be safe from the pressure of commercial exploitation.

In the past we have had far too modest ideas of the areas which should be set aside and protected for national parks. The existing parks are often too circumscribed to protect the native wildlife. For wilderness consists of far more than an area in which trees are not cut and roads are not built. It comprises the entire plant and animal life in what our scientists now call a *biotic* unit. That is no true wilderness which is so small that the animals may stray carelessly across the border where they may be shot down by the predatory hunter. The true wilderness must be large enough to protect its game as well as its forests and streams and ground cover. It must be large enough to serve a considerable number of people and yet give them a sense of distance from the inhabited places of the earth and from each other.

We have thought in too limited terms. Before it is too late we should see that the national parks which belong to all the people, not only take care of their owners and stockholders who travel along the paved highway to see what can be seen from a car window, but also meet the need of the urge for the primitive which many of our people inherit from their recent ancestors and long to indulge. Perhaps if these areas are numerous enough and large enough to serve our people without crowding, they may offer a promise of uplifting and prolonging our civilization and culture.

MAGNIFICENT MOUNTAINS OF THE NORTHWEST

PROBABLY a drive on a circuit which would take in all the national parks, not to mention the monuments, would easily equal the distance around the world. To the marathon motorist anything is possible, and no doubt it would be possible to "tag" each park and monument, drive over its roads and then take to the highway again—all within a few months. But the kaleidoscopic memories would be blurred and no one could hope, in so hurried a trip, to reach anything like a true understanding of the national parks or to receive the poignant aesthetic enjoyment and high inspirational uplift which are inherent in the parks.

It is possible, however, to visit a number of national parks on a single summer trip without mental and spiritual indigestion. Indeed, one of the best ways of becoming familiar with the national parks is to visit them in convenient regions.

At Mt. Rainier in 1938, the writer met a businessman and his wife, crowding fifty, who had been spending their vacations for twenty-five years in the national parks—only one or two in a season. When their children were young they brought them along. Now that all were married or settled in their own pursuits, this happy, vigorous couple were having a sort of silver wedding trip. They drove in their car and stopped in the camps where they felt that they could stay as long as they desired. They joined in all the scheduled trips and activities. They knew the flowers and the trees of the western mountains and could compare the qualifications of the ranger naturalists with others they had heard. They were good walkers, and in addition to the guided automobile caravans and hiking trips, they struck out for themselves with the convenient trail maps supplied in the parks. They evidently felt that they were visiting each summer one or two of their fine summer estates, in which their collective ownership made possible excellent facilities for their pleasure and profit. They not only enjoyed the parks they visited; they were discriminatingly appreciative of all they saw on these truly American journeys.

The first region selected for our imaginary journey lies in the extreme northwest corner of the continental United States, where magnificent mountains are as common as blackberries.

OLYMPIC NATIONAL PARK

Our first visit will be made to the Olympic Peninsula, where a national park was created by Congress in June of 1938. The Olympic Peninsula roughly has a hundred-mile frontage on the Pacific Ocean. From the extreme northwest point of Cape Flattery to Port Townsend on the north almost another hundred miles of waterfront lies on Juan de Fuca Strait. The Peninsula is separated from Everett, Seattle, and Tacoma by Puget Sound and the Hood Canal. Projecting eastward from the Pacific Ocean is Grays Harbor, which cuts the Peninsula from the mainland on the South. The Peninsula may be reached by motor road and ferry from Seattle and other western Washington towns. It may be reached from Olympia, the capital of the State, and from Oregon and California by the Olympic Highway which encircles the mountains.

Within this modern highway lies one of the most interesting and alluring wilderness mountain-and-valley areas remaining in this country. Ben Thompson, writing in *Planning and Civic Comment*, described this enchanted land: "Almost rimmed with the mills and smoke and noise of Puget Sound's industrial communities, it is still a wild land. Dark and jungle-like forests cover the lowlands and extend far up the narrow river bottoms. Successions of steep ridges under shaggy forest robes reach up to the central mass of tossed and jumbled peaks. On clear days its snowy crests stand out white and silent.

"Each summer, meadows of wild flowers creep up the slopes after the receding snow, while down in the lowlands a cougar stalks the river trail, leaving the tracks of his soft pads in the mud. In autumn, elk bugle through the woods, while the mountain beavers, high on the hillside, survey the coming of winter. Then snow settles down on the mountains, rain drenches the lowlands, and it is again an island of solitude."

John Muir first saw Mt. Olympus from the deck of a boat some fifteen miles south en route to Alaska in 1879. Again in 1890, from the same vantage point, he remarked: "The sail to Port Townsend is very interesting on account of the beauty and grandeur of the scenery, especially of the Olympic Mountains, which rise to eight thousand feet above the blue waters, with picturesquely sculptured summits and long withdrawing slopes heavily clad with spruce and fir." These mountains do, indeed, present to the eye from certain high lookouts a dramatic skyline, but one traveling on the Olympic Highway would have no idea of the beauty hidden within the charmed circle of the interior of the ring road, for this highway passes through many sad cut-over regions, patches of second growth, and occasionally into virgin forests; it is so located that the interior mountains can seldom be seen.

The Peninsula was almost entirely covered with dense forests at one time, except where the high craggy peaks emerged above the timber line. Once it was a veritable lumberman's paradise. Muir remarked in one of his journal entries that many of the Sierra forests had remained intact because it was easier to bring timber a thousand miles by water from the Northwest than fifty miles from the California mountains. At any rate, 130 years after the Lewis and Clark Expedition into the Northwest, such vast areas of forest have been cut that the remaining stands in the heart of the Olympic Peninsula have achieved a scarcity value and become so unique as to qualify for national-park status.

It is now thirty-five years since a bill almost passed Congress to create the Elk National Park on the Olympic Peninsula "for the purpose of preserving the elk, game, fish, birds, animals, timber and curiosities therein." The bill, introduced in 1904, passed the House and failed in the Senate during the last hours of the session. Bills to create a game preserve failed in 1906 and 1908. Finally, in the closing days of his administration, President Theodore Roosevelt set aside the Mt. Olympus National Monument of something over 600,000 acres. In the meantime, the forest reserves were transferred from the Department of the Interior to the Department of Agriculture; in 1907 the name was changed to national forests. The elk were protected by state law, according to an account by Dr. Theodore Palmer in *Civic Comment:* "For a quarter of a century the dual arrangement continued under which the elk were protected by the state law, while the range was protected by the National Monument act as administered by the Forest Service."

In 1916, President Wilson, on the recommendation of the Forest Service, in an effort to provide timber for ship-building to win the war, by Executive Order reduced the Monument to less than half its original size. Then in 1933 came two more changes. Under a new state game law, the Game Commission of Washington authorized an open season on elk for six days and killing was permitted for the first time since 1905. It was in this year, too, that President Franklin D. Roosevelt by Executive Order transferred the Mt. Olympus National Monument, along with other national monuments, from the jurisdiction of the U. S. Forest Service to that of the National Park Service. No hunting is permitted in national monuments, but the protection of the high winter range for the elk was not enough. The movement to create a national park was revived. In the meantime each year more people were hiking or packing into the interior wilderness, and they wanted to see the area made into a national park. As might have been expected, perhaps, there was bitter opposition to enlarging the national monument to national-park proportions, and thus taking land from the economic uses permitted in national forests.

In *American Forests* for June, 1936, John B. Yeon presented the case for the park. The plan of the Forest Service, Mr. Yeon declared, "in accordance with the basic provisions of national forest legislation, has given prior consideration to the economic utilization of the timber. Preservation has been designated only where it does not materially interfere with the conversion of the forest into lumber. The areas reserved are for the most part economically worthless." On the other hand, "the plan for the Olympics advocated by the Park Service aims to add a solid block of forest to the solid reservation of the existing monument and incorporate both in the national park." This in contrast to the fingers of forest open for harvesting proposed by the Forest Service. Mr. Yeon continued: "This plan (of the Park Service) in accordance with the basic provisions of national park legislation gives prior consideration to the preservation of the area's natural geographic and biotic features. The scenic, recreational, educational and inspirational resources of the region, and the requirements for their use and protection without depletion, are the factors which have shaped the program. The application of this plan would result in the permanent survival of an unmodified forest on a scale commensurate with the mountains it covers and with the giant individual specimens it contains. It would save a forest landscape and not merely samples of trees. The natural aspect of the area would remain intact—the original horizons as well as foregrounds and the infinite details which compose the whole."

Mr. Yeon warned us that "The forests of the Olympics will not be commonplace again. No other large area in this zone will probably ever be held undisturbed for the five centuries required for such a forest to mature. If this were done, however, and every trace of modification eventually eroded or rotted away, this future forest would still be different in historic and scientific category from the one still flourishing in the Olympics today. Here is the culmination of an incalculably old growth process, far older, perhaps, than the combined age of all its living trees. The present forest has an ancient lineage; it is in the line of direct descent from the first plant forms growing in the earliest Olympic soils. The 'thrilling succession from the infinite which cannot be returned once continuity has been severed' is a real but intangible attribute which will be effaced from this area once it is disturbed and absent forever from subsequent forests of modern origins."

Fortunately, the fight was won for scenic and inspirational values when the Wallgren Bill of 1938 became a law establishing a defined national park of 634,000 acres, with authority to the President to add lands until the national park may include 892,292 acres. In this Olympic National Park, we find then, as described by John Yeon in 1936: "The forested valleys and canyons, in conjunction with the adjacent Alpine regions, result in a combination which enhances the interest of all features beyond what the component parts would, if isolated, possess in themselves. The area is surrounded on three sides . . . by salt water. It is almost an island—a miniature continent in itself. Within this area, rivers have their source and major being before their confluence with the ocean. The circuit of moisture, lifting from the sea, detained in glaciers, and flowing through streams and rivers back to the sea, is complete, like a diagrammatic functioning model of the workings of earth forces, and almost within the range of observation from a single vantage point."

Secretary Ickes has publicly pledged the Department of the Interior to the preservation of this wilderness area. There will be no roads into the interior. But that does not mean that visitors may not see the mountains and the forested valleys to advantage. The headquarters of the National Park Service, instead of being in the park, will be built on forty acres of land, adjoining Port Angeles, given to the Park Service by Clallam County. From Port Angeles travelers may drive out to some of the idyllic inns on the shores of Crescent Lake, or they may stay at the settlements at Sol Duc or Olympic Springs, from where the northern valleys may be explored. The rather rough road along Hurricane Ridge will undoubtedly be improved, and perhaps extended. From the ridge may be seen Mt. Olympus, with its blue glacier and the galaxy of snowy peaks around it. From the Olympic Highway on the East a road leads up the Hoh Valley to Jackson. From here one may walk as far up the valley as strength and inclination permit, remembering always that the very essence of the Hoh forests is their isolation from highways and motor traffic. In the Hoh are some of the largest Douglas firs in existence. One named for Colonel Graves will some day be a fitting monument to a former Chief Forester who has rendered to the country a fine service in vision and educational leadership.

Visitors may stop at the hotel at Lake Quinault at the southeastern corner of the park. They may drive up to Graves Creek Inn in the southern part of the park, though their hearts may be saddened by the cut-over lands which border the road and by the constant stream of trucks bearing giant firs to market. From Graves Creek Inn visitors may drive a short distance to the Quinault River where the road now ends, and let us hope, where it will always end. There is a high-hung foot and horse bridge across the Quinault at this point, and visitors should by all means walk across it. The banks of the river are almost perpendicular and the rocks are padded and tufted with delicate maidenhair ferns. A lovelier fern exhibit could not be imagined. As the trail traverses the stream up the valley, many of the misshapen trees are seen to be covered with green moss, which gives the region an unearthly aspect and justifies the name "Enchanted Valley." Just north of the old Monument line, about eleven miles from Graves Creek Inn, is an inn to which all food and supplies must be brought by pack train. From the Enchanted Valley one may ride horseback (or walk) across Anderson Pass and out along the Dosewallips to reach a highway which intersects the Olympic Highway on the east side of the park. Or the trip may be made in reverse action.

At the southeast corner the access road will probably be extended to the head of Lake Cushman.

One especially interesting pack trip may be made from Sol Duc

Photograph—C. Frank Brockman Courtesy—American Forests

MT. RAINIER WINTER SPORTS

Photograph—Asahel Curtis   Courtesy—Portfolio, American Planning and Civic Association

MAJESTIC   MOUNT   RAINIER

Springs, and along the Bogachiel ridge to the ranger station on the top of Bogachiel by way of Seven-lake Basin. Often on the snow-banks elk may be seen resting in the lazy summer afternoons. A trail from Bogachiel leads to the Blue Glacier on Mt. Olympus. There is also a trail down the south side of the mountain into the Hoh Valley far below. For this ride down the switchbacks from the ranger station to the floor of the valley more than a mile lower in altitude, one needs good knees, for the steady pressure to hold the saddle for two or three hours, with never a step up, but always down, is a little trying on the "tenderfoot." Once in the upper Hoh Valley, no matter how tired, the traveler is so consumed with admiration for the lofty and aged Douglas firs and other forest masterpieces that weariness is soon forgotten.

There are many trails and trips over the High Divide, the Low Divide, and up the Queets. Of course there is much rain on the Peninsula, particularly on the west side, and many of the pack-train parties are overtaken by rain, but the mountain clubs of the Northwest continue to hike and ride into these delectable mountains, and the American Forestry Association has annually, in recent years, scheduled popular pack-train trips into the Olympics.

Without roads which will cross the heart of this fine national park, but with half a dozen or more access roads which will bring visitors to points where they may find comfortable accommodations and with comparatively short walks see some part of the forested valleys, with one high ride on Hurricane Ridge from which the whole range may be seen, there will be ample facilities for the motorist to see and enjoy the park without ruining its wilderness character. And the park will be increasingly popular for the sturdy hiker and the untiring horseback rider. Riding along in an automobile or walking along the trails in the valleys, besides all the small, scampering animals, one may frequently see coveys of grouse, with their quail-like waddle, glide away into the forest, and occasionally, as a special treat, one may watch the stately iridescent pheasants, with their brilliant hues, walk in solemn procession across the stage with its dark evergreen drops.

Now that the long-standing controversies about the future of the heart of the Olympics are settled and the shouting and the tumult have died, we, the people, may well picture to ourselves the kingdom which we have inherited. William Harrison Peters, in April, 1936, *American Forests* gave us some unforgettable word sketches: "Beginning at the salt water where the Pacific roars against the rugged coast, and at the sparkling blue of the Strait of Juan de Fuca and Hood Canal, these wonderful forests climb to an elevation of 4,000 feet above the sea. They completely encircle the Olympic Mountains, a green unbroken belt fifty miles wide and more than 200 miles in circumference. Inside, and above the inner circumference of this sloping belt of rugged, timber-covered foothills, Mt. Olympus rears its peak of basalt and ice 8,000 feet above the surrounding seas.

"Between the belt of dense forest growth and the snow and ice of the high peaks, lies an area of delectable open meadows, grass covered, dotted with alpine lakes and spotted with clumps of mountain hemlock, alpine fir and an occasional Alaska cedar.

"From the glacier-covered peaks of the Olympics pour scores of streams. Born in clear mountain springs or tiny glacial lakes, they join to form brawling creeks which unite to send wide rivers flowing quietly through forest-covered valleys to the sea. These streams abound in fish, and the river valleys, broad and flat, shelter great herds of Roosevelt elk. The mountain ridges furnish sanctuary and browse for many deer; bears are plentiful. Grouse and pheasant occur in all parts of the region.

"During the summer months, the area at timberline is a carpet of alpine flowers. There are asters, violets, gentians, phlox, bluebell, hellebore, avalanche lily, *Erythronium parviflorum*, a sturdy flower that in early spring pushes through the receding snow drifts to bloom, a dozen varieties of the sedum, the 'hen and chicks' and 'stonecrop' of the natives, vermilion Indian paintbrush, and dozens of others of equal beauty and interest."

Major Owen A. Tomlinson in 1937, in the *American Planning and Civic Annual* gave a fine description of the Olympics: "Burdened with glistening and still active glaciers, never completely explored, the snowy white of the taller peaks contrasts with the luxuriant verdure of their evergreen slopes. The region surpasses in massive grandeur many more famous but less beautiful tourist territories. . . . Moulded by glaciation in a period approximated at some 20,000 years ago, the resultant spectacular topography is a marvel of distinctive, rugged and isolated domain, with many peaks unnamed and unclimbed."

Photograph—Asahel Curtis   Courtesy—Portfolio, American Planning and Civic Association

APPROACH TO MT. RAINIER

AVALANCHE LILIES AT MT. RAINIER

Photograph—Department of the Interior   Courtesy—Portfolio, American Planning and Civic Association

PARADISE INN IS OPEN
THE YEAR ROUND

Courtesy—American Civic Annual

PARADISE VALLEY,
MT. RAINIER

COMMUNITY HOUSE IN PARADISE VALLEY

Photographs—Department of the Interior   Courtesy—Portfolio, American Planning and Civic Association

The Sitka spruce, one of the great tree species, is preserved in the Olympic National Park; also Douglas fir, Western red cedar, and the smaller white fir and hemlock, "with age-old coatings of moss, hanging heavily to soften the solid contours of the branches." "Heavy tropic-like vegetation—the forest within a forest—disappears miraculously, leaving only huge trunked forest monarchs, then as suddenly reappears. Elsewhere, ferns carpet the trail and forest floor. Heavy-reeded waterways break suddenly into broad, pebbled expanses."

Surely future generations will rise up and call blesséd this generation which acted before it was too late to save these pedigreed forests of Douglas fir, Sitka spruce, Alaska cedar and hemlock!

MT. RAINIER

From the Olympic Peninsula visitors may easily go to Mt. Rainier, which has been a national park since 1899. It required considerable foresight to set aside Mt. Rainier as a national park forty years ago, looking forward from that year; but looking back from this year, we now know that so stupendous a mountain required a larger rim of protection. In 1931 the eastern boundary was extended to the summit of the Cascade Range and fifty odd square miles were added to the 325 square miles already in the park. The park is roughly in the form of a square with the mountain peak, 14,408 feet high, a little to the left of the center, and its glaciers radiating out in some places to points only three or four miles within the boundaries.

One may enter the park by highway from the southwest corner by the Nisqually River entrance, and drive by way of Longmire Springs, where the National Park Service has its headquarters office, to Paradise Valley, high on the slopes of the mountain. At Longmire there is quite a settlement, including a museum, an inn, a public camp, store, cafeteria, gasoline station, and post office.

It is here that Major Tomlinson has presided for enough years to make his name synonymous with Rainier. The Major is a quiet, retiring ex-army officer. He is thoroughly imbued with the Mather national-park ideals, and he knows the Washington mountains like a book.

[123]

The road to Paradise Valley passes close to the Nisqually Glacier. For many years this road was a single, one-way controlled highway on which travel was permitted only at certain hours; but now it is possible to use the widened improved highway at pleasure. At Paradise there is also a settlement, including an inn, a lodge, cabins, public camps beautifully situated, store, gasoline station, post office and community house where nightly lectures are given.

One may enter the northwest corner of the park by the Carbon River Road and find a ranger station and public campgrounds. On the east side of the park there is a very beautiful highway, called the Mather Memorial Parkway, which gives access to the Yakima Park section of the park both from the north and from the southeast. As this parkway comes through the gate, at a lookout within the park, there is an unforgettable view of Rainier which is more breath-taking than any to be seen from other vantage points. The afternoon sun on the icy mantle of Rainier gives the effect of a crystal-studded garment, faceted to catch every ray of light. At Yakima Park there are to be found cabins, cafeteria, camp (especially well located), and other facilities, including a picturesque campfire and amphitheatre which is well patronized when the park rangers give illustrated talks each evening during the summer months.

There is an entrance at the southeast corner to the Ohanapecosh Ranger Station, where there are a lodge, cabins, camp, and hot baths.

The ascent of Mt. Rainier is only for the hardy. Though the mountain was first seen and named by Captain George Vancouver, of the British Royal Navy, in 1792, it was not until 1870 that its summit was reached. In that year two successful ascents were made, but it was not until 1883 that the summit was reached for the third time. Today, of course, ascents are quite common, but except for experienced mountaineers, would-be climbers must take guides with them. The National Park Service, in its pamphlet on the park, has stated plainly that "Mount Rainier is a difficult peak to climb. The route to the summit is not a definitely marked path. Dangerously crevassed ice covers a large proportion of the mountain's flanks, and the steep ridges between glaciers are composed of treacherous crumbling lava and pumice. Weather on the mountain is fickle. Midsummer snow storms, always accompanied by fierce gales, rise with unexpected suddenness." All these obstacles, of course, make the ascent all the more exciting and desirable to those who do take the trip, and one of the special lures of the park is the climbing of Mt. Rainier.

The park offers many interesting trips for those who do not attempt to scale the summit. There are five access highways through four main entrances, with less than sixty miles of highway in the entire park. But there are 240 miles of trails leading through and to some of the most charming high country in the park system. From the Nisqually entrance there is an excellent highway, within the boundaries of the park, leading north some fifteen miles to Klapatche Park. From this highway trails lead to Indian Henry's Hunting Ground, where there is a gorgeous display of wild flowers in the summer months. A trail skirts the Tahoma Glacier, and another leads to the Payallup Glacier.

There are innumerable walking and riding trips from Paradise Valley. It is an easy walk up to the Muir Shelter Cabin, where the mountaineers who expect to scale the summit spend the early hours of the night, before they start on their chilly, early-morning climb hoping to see the sunrise from the top. Muir Shelter, which is at the 10,000-foot elevation, is some 4,500 feet above Paradise, but the climb requires no special skill, although those who have not the "wind and the limb" may secure horses, and ride. There are excellent views all along the trail, and a feeling of having reached the snowy heights at Camp Muir. Leading out from Paradise there is a regular network of trails on which may be seen any summer day literally hundreds of people, young and old, climbing vigorously or sauntering along at their free will, enjoying the fine views and the exercise in the high, clear air.

On the guided trips, the glaciers are explained, the flowers and trees identified. Anyone who takes all the guided trips and who travels all the mapped trails on foot or horseback will certainly become well informed about the geology, flora and fauna of the park and have excellent opportunities for aesthetic enjoyment, to be found in few places in the world.

Running entirely around the mountain is the Wonderland Trail, which, with its various ramifications, is from a hundred to a hundred and forty miles in the circuit. Hikers, by carrying sleeping bag and food, can make a shelter each night, and so in a week or ten days the mountain can be seen from the highlands from every angle and the lower end of every glacier can be examined. The trail from Sunrise (Yakima Park) to Paradise is full of surprises. It runs along Frying Pan Creek to Summerland, where the wild flowers flourish, cutting across the Frying Pan Glacier and skirting the Ohanapecosh Glacier, past Indian Bar Shelter to the Nickel Creek Ranger Station and across the spectacular Canyon Bridge where, because of the great depth below and the roar of the falling water, riders are asked to dismount; up Stevens Creek past Louise Lake and Nerada Falls to the Paradise Highway. In July there is usually heavy snow on the passes and covering the Frying Pan Glacier, which lies far below. When the writer made the journey, the ranger at Nickel Creek had placed little red flags over the several miles of snow to indicate the safe places for the horses' feet. While one is not as near the summit of Rainier in crossing the Frying Pan Glacier as at Muir Shelter Cabin on the Paradise side, one feels nearer the mountain tops of everlasting snow, because as far as the eye can reach there is nothing but the shining whiteness of the snow and ice in sight. For the "wilderness feeling," this two-day hiking or riding trip cannot easily be matched.

Rainier National Park gives adequate access roads to the motorists, who, with a moderate amount of walking, may see and enjoy the mountain. But its real glory is seen from the trails, short and long, provided for hikers and riders. The number that annually take advantage of the trail facilities is an evidence that the American public is becoming "trail minded" and relearning the use of the human body for walking purposes!

Time was when Rainier closed up shop in winter. Not so today. Since skiing has taken this country by a storm as unaccountable as the black tulip craze in Holland, no snow field is complete without its amateur skiers, no fiction magazine without its ski story, no outdoor periodical without its article on skiing and skiing equipment. The sports shops of the United States which a few years ago were barren of any sort of ski equipment are now well stocked and apparently selling their stock. Rainier is one of the famous skiing places in the United States. Even in the dead of winter when cars can only be driven to a point a mile and a half below Paradise Inn, the Inn is kept open and the ski enthusiasts cheerfully pad up the mountain to claim their accommodations.

Photograph—Department of the Interior Courtesy—Portfolio, American Planning and Civic Association

THE BLUE WATERS OF CRATER LAKE

[127]

CROSSING A CREVASSE IN
THE CASCADE RANGE

Photograph—John W. Murray
Courtesy—Appalachia

MT. BAKER IN THE
WASHINGTON CASCADES

Photographs—Aubrey R. Watzek
Courtesy—American Planning and Civic Annual

MT. MAGIC
IN THE CASCADES
NEAR LAKE CHELAN

Fortunately for those who love scenery, skiing does no damage to the summer scenery and provides an exciting and absorbing winter sport. Conservationists generally, however, discourage any sort of paraphernalia to haul the happy skiers up the mountain, as a permanent scar on natural scenery.

Mt. Rainier is unique. It has, according to Frank Brockman, writing in *American Forests*, "upon its broad flanks the largest glacial system in the continental United States, exclusive of Alaska. Twenty-eight glaciers comprise this great system, forming an ice mantle nearly fifty square miles in area and covering thirteen per cent of the total area of Mount Rainier National Park." For scientific research, for summit-scaling, for skiing, for aesthetic enjoyment, for trail-tripping, and for inspirational contemplation, Mt. Rainier is a first-rate mountain.

CRATER LAKE

One may easily travel from Mt. Rainier to Crater Lake by way of Portland, then south to Medford and 80 miles along the Rogue River road into the park, or from Portland to Bend, Oregon, and 106 miles south to the park, with perhaps a detour to Diamond Lake. From the south one may enter from Klamath, either by the Klamath Highway or the Pinnacles Road. Rail and stage travel offer direct and convenient arrangements and, as there is a landing field at Medford, it is possible to hop from New York or Los Angeles with time-annihilating speed.

To state that the lake is six miles wide, 2,000 feet deep, with a circular shore line of 26 miles, that this vast volume of water depends upon precipitation into the giant bowl left from an exploding volcano, which is now preserved in a park covering 250 square miles, can give no faint suggestion of the beauty of Crater Lake. With all the lakes there are in the world and all the poetic phrases which have been used to describe them, it would seem that one little six-mile lake in the Cascades might not deserve much in the way of superlatives. There are different kinds of lake beauty and surroundings, and one would not want to miss the lovely mountain beauty of the Sierra lakes and meadows, nor the broad expanse of tree-fringed Tahoe, nor the severely chaste glacial lakes of Glacier National Park, nor the rugged isolation of Yellowstone Lake, lying high on the top of the continent, nor the shining necklace of glacial lakes at the foot of the Tetons. They all have beauties of their own. But the deep opalescent blue of Crater Lake is like some ethereal light borrowed from the skies. The ancients would have called it a creation of the gods. No one can look upon it and not be moved emotionally and spiritually. The setting of the highly painted lava cliffs gives it the appearance of some new gem more lovely than the sapphire set in some new combination of metals never before seen. The changing hues give it different aspects during the passing hours of the day from dawn to sunset. On rainy, cloudy days, the color is wiped out of the lake as though a palette knife had scraped off every bit of pigment and the secret of its beauty lost forever. Then the sunlight returns and the painting is again a work of rare genius, not to be understood but to be worshipped as an unduplicatable masterpiece of Nature.

From the rim drive one is led from one ecstasy to another. There is the view across the little lake of pure cerulean blue, with glimpses of Wizard Island casting its reflections in the mirror of the lake and of the Phantom Ship, sometimes appearing in full sail and sometimes suddenly disappearing with the change of lights. Early in the summer, when the snowplows have left high walls of snow and ice at the side of the road, the rim drive gives a nice feeling of remoteness.

The Indians had legends about the lake. One concerns Llao Rock, which rises nearly 2,000 feet above the lake level. As related in the national park bulletin on Crater Lake, according to the legends of the Klamath and Modoc Indians, "the mystic land of the Gaywas was the home of the great god Llao. His throne in the infinite depths of the blue waters was surrounded by giant crawfish, his warriors, who were able to lift great claws out of the water and seize too venturesome enemies on the cliff tops. War broke out with Skell, the god of the neighboring Klamath marshes. Skell was captured and his heart used for a ball by Llao's monsters. But an eagle, one of Skell's servants, captured it in flight, and a coyote, another of Skell's servants, escaped with it; and Skell's body grew again around his living heart. Once more he was powerful and once more he waged war against the god of the lake. Then Llao was captured; but he was not so fortunate.

Upon the highest cliff his body was quartered and cast into the lake and eaten by his own monsters under the belief that it was Skell's body. But when Llao's head was thrown in, the monsters recognized it and would not eat it. Llao's head still lies in the lake, and white men call it Wizard Island. The cliff where Llao was quartered is named Llao Rock."

Crater Lake was discovered at least three times in the fifties and sixties before it received its present name in 1869. Following a trip to Crater Lake in 1885 by William Gladstone Steel, Professor Joseph Le Conte, and others, President Cleveland in 1886 issued a proclamation withdrawing ten townships, including Crater Lake, from settlement. Crater Lake National Park was created by Congress and approved by President Theodore Roosevelt in 1902.

In this national park, which contains one of the most beautiful single objects in the whole system and one which depends for its appreciation on its emotional and spiritual appeal, it is curious that the scientific information is the most complete. The Sinnott Memorial, which was constructed of native stone on Victor Rock, just inside the rim of the crater, offers a fine balcony from which to examine the lake and its surroundings. Through the means of high-powered field glasses, visitors are enabled to see "close-ups" of the walls of the lake and read in the legends at the glass of the geological history and present composition of each feature of the landscape. The large relief map of the Crater Lake Region receives a great deal of interested attention from visitors. Carefully prepared displays are on view in the exhibit room. The interpretation of science here has been managed with a great deal of skill and has been kept simple enough not to leave the visitors with scientific indigestion.

Crater Lake has, in common with the rest of the Southern Cascades, a wide variety of wild flowers. Over 500 flowering plants and ferns are listed. Many of these may be found in the Castle Crest Wild Flower Garden, near the National Park Headquarters, three miles from the rim. One of the attractions of the park is found in the brilliantly hued flowers. In the open sunny spaces the flaming fireweed, which flourishes in most of the western parks, reaches a climax of burning glory. The principal trees are ponderosa pines, mountain hemlock, a variety of pines, Shasta red fir, Engelmann spruce, and Douglas fir. Oaks, cottonwoods, and aspens give fresh young green to the spring and brilliant foliage to the autumn.

In spite of the highways and crowds of people coming into the park, many regions are wild enough to give cover to the smaller wild animals—deer, elk, bear, marmots, conies, minks, weasels, martens, beavers, badgers, porcupines, flying squirrels, and many others. In addition to the smaller birds there are to be found falcons, ospreys, golden and bald eagles, and horned owls.

Fish were planted in Crater Lake fifty years ago, and today the lake teems with rainbow and steelhead trout.

There are many interesting activities at Crater Lake. There is the camera hike for camera fans. There is the boat trip to Wizard Island, made by most visitors, and many like to go out in rowboats both by daylight and in the moonlight, when the mysterious lake, with its floating islands and its darkly shadowed cliffs, presents a scene of unutterable beauty.

It was at Crater Lake that the first annual ski races were held, and there is a permanent Crater Lake Ski Club. Since 1935 the roads have been kept clear of snow and the park has been open throughout the winter.

According to David Canfield, "the beauty of the park in winter . . . is in many respects, unequalled. The crowning spectacle, of course, is Crater Lake with its indescribable blue, nestling in a circle of high white-robed cliffs. The heavily burdened conifers with their magnificent mantles of snow are a never-ending delight; the fantastic curves and snow masses of the smaller trees cause one to marvel at the artistry of nature. The drifts offer mute testimony to the force and vagaries of the wind."

Either entering or departing, or as a loop trip, every park visitor should drive along the Pinnacles Road and see the peculiar formations in Wheeler Creek Canyon.

One should at least see the clock round at Crater Lake, and a longer stay would allow for interesting explorations and, even more important, for seeing the changing colors of the lake and its surroundings.

THE WILDERNESS WAY IN THE CASCADES

A project which has appealed to the imagination of the lovers of wilderness and mountain climbing has been fostered by Clinton

MEADOW LAKE AND
MT. SHUKSAN

IN THE NORTHERN
CASCADES

GLEAMING "PAH-TO"—
INDIAN NAME FOR MT. ADAMS
SECOND HIGHEST PEAK
IN WASHINGTON

Photograph—U. S. Forest Service
Courtesy—American Forests

[133]

MT. BAKER, THE SILENT SENTINEL

Churchill Clarke, of Pasadena, California, in the Pacific Crest Trail, which, by linking together many existing trails, now runs from the Canadian line to Mexico, a total distance of 2,300 miles, of which all but 175 miles is within the borders of twenty national forests and five national parks. Eight hundred and fifty miles of the Pacific Crest Trail lie within the mountains of the Northwest. Robert Foote, writing in *American Forests*, has explained that the first 450 miles comprise the Cascade Crest Trail which "runs south through the most primitive and unexplored region in the United States. The Cascade Range, of Washington, is broken into heavily timbered gorges and ice-streaked ridges, above which rise mighty glacier peaks. To cover this trail requires forty or more days of hard tramping, over twenty-two mountain passes and around five glacier peaks and Mt. Rainier National Park. The Cascade Crest runs entirely through wilderness except for small recreation centers near Mt. Baker, Keechelus Lake and Mt. Rainier Park.

"In Oregon the Cascades are more gentle than in Washington, and the Oregon Skyline is not so difficult, is generally in better condition and well marked, crossing only four passes. Nevertheless, this 410 miles requires thirty-eight days of foot travel. The three outstanding peaks to be passed, Mt. Hood, Mt. Jefferson, and the Three Sisters, are strongly glacial though not entirely blanketed as is the case farther north. But in Oregon, the trail keeps to a higher average elevation than in Washington. Crater Lake National Park is an outstanding scenic area on this trail."

Considering that there still remains a most spectacular wilderness area in the United States in the Northern Cascades, and that the national parks as yet can claim only a little over 500 square miles in Rainier and Crater Lake, it is the opinion of many that a substantial Cascades National Park should be set aside for the pleasure and inspiration of the people of the United States. No mountain could be more impressive, perhaps, than Mt. Rainier, but Baker and Shuksan are not only stupendous in their scenic aspects, but they have a special personality.

Across the Skagit River lies a larger and even more remote region of glacial peaks, crests, and sharp cut valleys with turbulent streams and waterfalls, which will undoubtedly one day be brought into the national parks—not for development, but for preservation, and to provide more of that climax wilderness country which we are coming to demand for our civilization. No one who has ever walked or packed into this region could forget Lake Hart and Lake Lyman, lying in the shadow of the glacier-streaked peaks which are reflected in the glistening glass of their quiet waters, or the milky glacial waters of the Stehekin River, the heavenly blue of the gentians on Cloudy Pass, the marvelous views from Cascade Pass toward the Pacific, with the rugged crests of Mt. Magic like a fairy picture within a scene to the left, and endless crests on either side running toward the horizon beyond which are hidden Baker and Shuksan in a new climax. The roar of avalanches from the hanging glaciers, the calm of the capping glaciers, the quiet of the air where few birds sing, the rushing waters of the many streams, the rustling of the pines and spruces and cedars, the pungent scents of the virgin woods, the small filmy ferns, the tall coarse devil's walking canes, the fine ground cover of Oregon grape and mountain boxwood, with innumerable little flowers—all this and infinitely more will be the reward of those who travel by the trails of the Northern Cascades.

Hermann Ulrichs, writing in the February, 1937, *Sierra Club Bulletin*, has referred to the Northern Cascade section as the "last great stronghold of almost completely untouched primeval wilderness in the United States." He there maintained that "it will be regarded as the most spectacular, varied and truly Alpine of all our mountains." In amplification, Mr. Ulrichs drew an entrancing picture: "Wherever the climber goes, he is sure to see in some direction, one, if not several, of these solitary sentinels, often floating like a vision or mirage above the lower mists, strangely unreal and ethereal, and by their loftiness dwarfing the surrounding country. . . .

"It would be hard to imagine a more striking and felicitous contrast than that between this idyllic, really Arcadian country, of intimate beauty and delicacy, and the almost savage ruggedness and grandeur of the big peaks, the deep valleys far below, and the magnificent panoramas of distant snowy ranges glowing in the soft light."

THE PIONEER WESTERN PARKS

CALIFORNIA

A VISIT to the four California parks would make a very full summer. Indeed, there are those who go again and again to Yosemite or Sequoia and still feel that there are unknown places to explore and much to observe and learn. There must be, in the Coast Range, the Southern Cascades and the Sierra Nevada, within the State of California, at least 2,500 lineal miles of main mountain crests, of which 1,425 miles are in the Pacific Crest Trail. Less than 100 miles of these crests lie in national parks, passing through Lassen, Yosemite, and Sequoia National Parks.

LASSEN

Lassen Volcanic National Park, created by Congress in 1916, ten years after the land was withdrawn from settlement and declared a national monument by President Theodore Roosevelt, has been widely advertised because of the eruptions of 1914–15 and the sporadic outpourings of volcanic ash.

From the Northwest, Lassen may be reached from the highway running south from Crater Lake by way of Shasta and through Burney to the Manzanita Lake section. From the South, coming up through the rather hot Sacramento Valley, one may leave the main highway at Red Bluff for the road up the mountains to Mineral, a town outside the park boundaries, where the superintendent's headquarters are established. A good many visitors also come from the eastern California and Nevada towns by way of Susanville to Mineral, and then on to Lassen Volcanic Highway which connects with the Lassen Peak Loop Highway, a most spectacular drive during the summer months when the road is open for travel. The park highway leads by many springs and lakes around White Mountain and Summit Lake, over the devastated regions close by Lassen Peak, past Reflection Lake to Manzanita Lake, a distance of some fifty miles from Mineral. Every summer the road must be repaired from the snow and earth slides of the long winter before it is really safe for general use;

but those who are privileged to make the trip are very well repaid.

The park is an irregular rectangle ten by seventeen miles, containing 163 square miles. According to Collins and Lind in "Lassen Glimpses," published in 1929: "The area surrounding Lassen Peak and extending from it roughly for fifty miles east, south and west, and for some hundred miles north, was, back in geologic history during a period of strenuous volcanism, covered by lavas several thousands of feet in depth. These lavas issued principally from a main volcanic cone. By this action the terrain was wrought into the general shape of an immense dome, with the cone near the center and marking the highest point. Thus it may be seen that the Lassen Edifice, as this district is called, comprises a rather large section of country, owing its formation to the activities of a once tremendous volcano of which the present Lassen Peak is remaining evidence.

"Time, and Nature in her further processes of creation, caused decomposition of the lavas by which soil was formed. Forest growth commenced—to hold in storage moisture from the rains. Gradually in outward appearance this barren lava field was softened by the beauty of lake and forest, pleasant brooks and lovely flowers. The work of the old volcano was done, yet it has continued from time to time in less significant bursts of present-day activity, as though, like some old gentleman impelled by vanity, to voice in later generations the importance of past accomplishment.

"At the summit of the great dome, fringing the volcano and in reality part of it, though of secondary nature, were other lesser cones and lava vents whose discharge amplified the huge lava flows from their parent. As the main volcano went into decadence so did these others; and as glaciation, weathering and erosion followed, they were in part ground away. The result of this was the appearance of a unique area—a mass of remnant volcanoes interspersed with meadows, valleys, lakes, and streams. In part a fertile land of Nature's agriculture, contrasted by bits of present-day volcanics; all combined to make more interesting the magnificent spectacle of the old volcano rising in the midst. Perhaps nowhere in the world is the work of Nature in relation to physical geography evidenced more clearly or more interestingly. Here is a museum—a rather special treasure chest of Nature's varied handiwork."

LASSEN VOLCANIC NATIONAL PARK

Photographs—Department of the Interior   Courtesy—Portfolio, American Planning and Civic Association

IN JULY AND AUGUST
THE HOUSEKEEPING CABINS AT LASSEN NATIONAL PARK
ARE ALWAYS OCCUPIED

Of Lassen Peak itself, Collins and Lind have declared: "Lassen Peak is important in the geology of North America as a landmark denoting the fusion of lava Cascades with granite Sierra." It was Lassen Peak, formerly known as St. Joseph's Mountain, which served Peter Lassen as a guiding landmark when he piloted emigrants from Humboldt, Nevada, into the Sacramento Valley in California.

Lassen National Park offers not only a research area of great scientific importance but also an arena where interpretation of the processes of creation may be graphically illustrated for laymen. The climb up the mountain is not difficult and is undertaken by most of the able-bodied visitors. There are many other interesting phenomena in the park; the Cinder Cone and Lava Bed, which lie near Prospect Peak, and the blue waters of Butte Lake, in the northeast corner of the park, where there is a ranger station and a campground, attract many sightseers.

Again quoting from Collins and Lind: "The Cinder Cone country is a small district so startling and beautiful in an unusual way as to seem freakish. Almost a complete circle of ridges from six to eight thousand feet in height above sea level enclose a basin. . . . Evidence has been found to show that an ice pack over one thousand feet thick filled this basin during glacial times. Later it was the site of a rather large mountain lake." Several lava flows resulted in filling in most of the lake, leaving Snag and Butte Lakes.

The devastated area which resulted from the lava overflow from Lassen Crater in 1915 left a trail of destruction which will remain for many years, but reproduction is gradually being accomplished, and along the edges may be seen "young timber extending timidly into the barren flow."

Entirely apart from the marvels and wonders of Lassen National Park which draw visitors from all parts of the world, there is a very strong lure to the residents of a large area in the several adjoining States, which brings in camping and fishing parties who also make a point of climbing Lassen Peak and other mountains, who go on the various excursions around the park, and who also attend the nightly campfire programs conducted by the National Park Service. Lassen National Park renders an important educational and recreational service to the public.

[141]

YOSEMITE

From Lassen one may travel by way of the San Francisco Bay region, which in itself comprises many charming residence neighborhoods clustered around the Bay and its tributaries. Not far from Mt. Tamalpais, which overlooks the Golden Gate, is the charming Muir Woods—a national monument—which draws thousands of visitors annually to walk under its ancient coast redwoods (*Sequoia sempervirens*) and to sit in contemplation by the side of its crystal streams.

From the Bay region, or traveling directly south through Stockton, one may approach the El Portal entrance to Yosemite, either by train or by automobile. From El Portal one drives by the guarding rampart of El Capitan directly up the floor of the valley between the famous headlands on either side and within sight of the Bridalveil, Yosemite, and Ribbon Falls.

Many of those who visited the valley during the eighties and nineties, or even twenty-five or thirty years ago, resent the influx of people. Particularly on holidays during the summer are there great crowds to be found on the floor of the valley. At one time in the history of the park these crowds were more in evidence, though not larger, than they are today. Following carefully made plans the automobilists have been confined by inconspicuous barriers to the roads and to designated parking and camping places. The Yosemite is such a choice place on the earth's surface that it is natural for those who would like to enjoy it in solitude to resent the presence of so many of their fellow human beings in the valley. However, anyone who will look at the picture of Yosemite Valley (on page 22) will realize that great skill has been used to hide from view the hotels, inns, cabins, administration buildings, and living quarters of the park and hotel staffs, as well as twenty-three miles of highway. Indeed, it may be truthfully asserted that one may easily avoid the crowds in Yosemite Valley with a little care.

One of the pleasant experiences in Yosemite Valley is to drift around on the more secluded roads, including the road up to Mirror Lake at the head of the valley, in a car without a top, on a moonlight night. The span of starlit sky above the deep shadows of

AHWAHNEE HOTEL, YOSEMITE VALLEY

Photograph—Department of the Interior   Courtesy—Portfolio, American Planning and Civic Association

REAL SPORT ON SKIS IN YOSEMITE NATIONAL PARK

the cliffs, the sound of the rippling Merced River and the sight and sound of the falls, the reflection of sky and cliff in Mirror Lake, together with the cool, pure air of the Sierra, conspire to make such a night one to be remembered and treasured as long as one lives. While there are many beautiful places in the world, the Yosemite washed in moonlight seems to take on an ethereal quality which removes it from the Planet Earth.

One of the impressive ceremonies in Yosemite grew out of a chance revival of a rite, supposed to have been originated by James McCauley of the Mountain House. D. A. Curry, one of the pioneers in offering hospitality in the Yosemite, occasionally arranged, according to Dr. Carl Russell, to send some of the employees of Camp Curry to Glacier Point, over 3,000 feet above the floor of the valley, to build a fire and push it off. This came to be repeated until it was a nightly occurrence. Mr. Curry would call, "Hello," "All's well," and "Farewell," and the echo would be sent back from above. As the glowing embers of the fire are pushed over the cliff to float in the air until they turn to ash, there is always appropriate music. Visitors at the various campfires on the floor of the valley listen with rapt attention for the calls, the song, and the falling embers. No one who has witnessed it could ever forget Fire Fall!

Practically everyone who goes to Yosemite Valley drives or walks up to Glacier Point, where there are a Hotel and Mountain House, and from which one of the very best views in the park may be had. While Fire Fall is not as impressive at Glacier Point as from the floor of the valley, it is yet an experience to attend the campfire at the Point and to see the glowing embers pushed off the cliff while the calls come from below.

There are so many things to do and so many places to go in Yosemite that those who can, visit the park again and again. The valley, so beautiful and interesting in itself, is but a small part of the park. There are the drives to the three fine groves of Big Trees (*Sequoia gigantea*), the Tuolumne on the Big Oak Flat Road, the Merced Grove nearby, north of the valley, and the stately Wawona Grove south of the valley. There is the trip by way of the Tioga Road to Tuolumne Meadows and out over the Tioga Pass to Lake Tahoe, revealing some of the most spectacular Sierra country in Yosemite. Within the 1,176 square miles of the park there are 276 miles of roads and 688 miles of trails.

Hiking is very popular in California, due no doubt to the successful Sierra Club and other mountain groups. During the last fifteen years a series of High Sierra Camps has been developed which provide food and shelter for hikers in the form of a dormitory for men and one for women, and a mess and cook tent. With two exceptions, all food and supplies must be packed in by mules; but those who take the seven-day hiking trip need carry only a light pack with lunch and change of clothing. This makes it possible for many to take the swing around the back country who could not possibly pack bedding and food for seven days. But everyone gets up the trail to see Vernal and Nevada Falls.

Besides the wide range of accommodations in the valley, which run all the way from the de luxe service of the Ahwahnee, through the cottages, the tent cabins, and the dining-rooms at Camp Curry and other locations, to the public campgrounds, there are places to stay at Wawona Hotel, Big Trees Lodge, Glacier Point, Hotel and Mountain House, and Tuolumne Meadows Lodge.

It may be remembered that many of the mountains which John Muir loved to climb lie within the present Yosemite National Park—Hoffman and Lyell, not far from the valley, and a great galaxy of peaks and saw-tooth crests, wearing crystal gems of mountain lakes, which glorify the northern section of the park. On the southeastern boundary are Isber Pass, Triple Divide Peak, Fernandez and Chiquito Passes from which the Ritter-Minarets region, unfortunately outside the park, may be reached.

In addition to all the freedom of the park, to be claimed by those who ride or hike alone, there are many organized activities in Yosemite. Twice a day in summer there is an auto caravan led by a ranger naturalist who explains and interprets the interesting features in the park. There is a daily tour of the valley in open stages. A fine view of the valley is to be seen from the opening of the tunnel on the Wawona Road, just west of Bridalveil Fall. A ranger naturalist leads the seven-day hiking trips.

The Yosemite Museum was one of the first to be established, and furnishes interesting exhibits of the "geology, Indians, early history, trees, flowers, birds, and mammals" of Yosemite. The little group of native Yosemite Indians who demonstrate many

MOUNTAIN CAMP, MT. WHITNEY

From a sketch by T. Moran; from a lithograph in
Langley's "Researches on Solar Heat," 1884

Courtesy—Sierra Club Bulletin

SEQUOIA NATIONAL PARK

**AERIAL VIEW OF MT. WHITNEY AND
UPPER KERN BASIN
TABLE MOUNTAIN IN THE DISTANCE**

Photograph—Roy Curtis, Reno, Nevada
Courtesy—Sierra Club Bulletin

SEQUOIA GIGANTEA, WITH ITS DOMED CROWN,
DESCRIBED BY JOHN MUIR

Courtesy—American Forests

GENERAL SHERMAN TREE AT THE RIGHT, IN SEQUOIA
NATIONAL PARK. PROBABLY 4,000 YEARS OLD, THIS
GIANT IS 35 FEET IN DIAMETER AT ITS BASE
AND REACHES A HEIGHT OF 274 FEET

[148]

of the old customs back of the Museum, draw and hold the attention of all who visit them. There are campfire entertainments at various places in the park, but perhaps the most unique performance (outside of Fire Fall) is the nightly feeding of the bears, which may be observed across a stream. A ranger tells about the habits of the bears while the vast multitude watches their antics from a vantage point of safety.

Yosemite has become one of the most popular scenes of winter sports in the United States. Under its mantle of snow the valley is quite entrancing—no less so than it was when John Muir spent his first winter in the Sierra sixty years ago, for snow glorifies even the inevitable buildings and scars of occupation. The ice cone at the base of Upper Yosemite Fall which results from the frozen mist sometimes reaches a height of 300 feet and always adds to the winter beauty of the park. There are many skiing grounds in the park. According to the Yosemite bulletin, issued by the Park Service: "A new ski lodge, where ski equipment may be rented and light lunches and refreshments are served, is located at Badger Pass Meadow; elevation 7,300 feet, in the center of some of the finest skiing slopes in the West." Instructors are on hand to add to the skiing recruits. In the valley, which is protected from the winter winds, there are all kinds of skating events throughout the winter. There is a popular snowslide called "Ash Can Alley" down which merry boys and girls, yes, and men and women, slide in heavy tin pans which look exactly like the missing cover to the home ash-can.

Easter has come to be quite a day in Yosemite. A vast but breathlessly silent multitude assembles at Mirror Lake for the Sunrise Services. The first rays of the Sun as he touches with his magic golden wand the dusky ramparts of the valley and illumines the lake below, strike upon the eyes of the beholders with the dramatic force of a great annunciation. The high clear voices of the vested choir transform the valley into a great cathedral with flying buttresses and vaulted dome, transcending any mystic marvel of church architecture described by Henry Adams.

Yosemite is crowded on Easter, not only for the Sunrise Service, but also for the winter sports. Many of the visitors drive up to see the skiing and find it an exhilarating sight—the snowy mountain background, the bright costumes, the gay skiers.

[149]

Geologically, Yosemite Valley has a most dramatic history. To quote the national park bulletin: "The Yosemite Valley was cut to great depth in the first place by the Merced River, which flows through it and the Merced Canyon below. That river was repeatedly accelerated to torrential speed by the uplifts which in the course of many million years have given the Sierra Nevada its great height. Each time the river was accelerated it cut its channel deeper, and so at last it fashioned a narrow V-shaped canyon over 2,000 feet in depth. The lesser side streams, meanwhile, were unable to cut so fast, and as a consequence their valleys were left hanging high above the bottom of the canyon. The original Yosemite Canyon thus became adorned by many cascades of great height and beauty.

"Then came the Ice Age, and the Yosemite Canyon was invaded by a mighty glacier that descended slowly but irresistibly from the crest of the range. During the climax of the Ice Age this glacier filled the canyon literally to the brinks, and extended down to the site of El Portal. It reached within 700 feet of the crown of Half Dome, and overrode Glacier Point to a depth of 700 feet. Forcing its way with tremendous power, it gradually widened the narrow V-shaped canyon to a broad U-shaped trough. It cut back the sloping sides to sheer cliffs and transformed the cascades to leaping water-falls. It also added to the depth of the valley, excavating a lake basin in its rock floor. When at last the glacier melted away it left a lake 5½ miles long. But that lake did not endure, for the Merced River brought down vast quantities of sand and gravel, and in the course of time filled the lake completely, and produced the level parklike floor which adds so much to the visitor's enjoyment of the Valley." In comparison with such mighty public works, Boulder Dam and Grand Coulee seem ineffective and ephemeral!

From a motor-car window, from the back of a horse, or afoot, the Yosemite offers deep interest and intense pleasure for those who love the Sierra. The great variety of wild flowers always excites admiration. The actual tramping of feet and the processes of occupation have indeed destroyed the brilliant flower gardens of John Muir's day, but with management many of these have been restored, and in the mountains and valleys of the park, where there is little traffic, the flowers of Yosemite are still among the loveliest in the Sierra. With the variations of elevation there are zones of plant types. Definitely, the national park bulletin has directed attention to the fact that "Five life zones are represented characterized by a brush belt (chaparral) with its manzanita and wild lilac (*Ceanothus* sp.) interspersed with live oaks and the Digger pine forest at the lowest altitudes and grading into yellow mountain pine, and then to a timber line forest of mountain hemlock and white-barked pine. Lichens, mosses, and a few alpine flowering plants characterize the alpine-arctic zone. . . .

"Flowering plants in great profusion add new beauty with the advancing season. Early spring marks the flowering of the tree dogwood, followed by such shrubs as the Philadelphus (wild syringa), western azalea, and pink spiraea. Whole mountainsides blaze with ocean spray (*Holodiscus discolor*). Meadows at lower elevations start white with death camas and mariposa lilies (*Calochortus* sp.); turn to yellow with evening primroses (*Oenothera* sp.), buttercups, and goldenrod; blue with lupines and larkspur; to red with Indian paintbrush (*Castilleia* sp.); and finally pink with fireweed, pussy paws (*Calyptridium*), and *Lessingia*. The snow plant (*Sarcodes sanguinea*) and pine drops (*Pterospora andromeda*) are common saprophytic plants of the pine forests, the former appearing like a bright red giant asparagus tip. . . . On the highest peaks are found two beautiful plants, the Sierra primrose and the sky pilot (*Polemonium eximium*). Here also cassiope, a white heather, replaces the pink one which grows at slightly lower elevations."

Only lovers of the high places on the face of the earth can feel the thrill that comes from crossing the lingering snowbanks at the summits of passes along the trail and then finding bright beds of the lovely Sierra primrose and acres of the modest cassiope clustering close to the ground around the rocks and shale of the mountainside. The streams of Yosemite are well stocked with fish, and the Waltonians may whip the remote waters of the park or fish quietly in the rivers and tributaries of the Merced Valley.

One wonders if Yosemite Valley and the High Sierra country around it might not serve as a prototype for the mythical Garden of Eden. At any rate, he who has not seen Yosemite has not yet been to Carcassonne!

SEQUOIA AND GENERAL GRANT

The Sequoia and General Grant National Parks were, of course, created primarily to preserve the Big Trees without particular consideration of the general scenic values likely to be included. In Sequoia is the famous Giant Forest, so named by John Muir and described by him as no one since has equaled. Of the long hike he made with "Brownie" the mule, down the crest of the Sierra, we have heard much. In his book on "Our National Parks," he has recounted: "Day after day, from grove to grove, canyon to canyon, I made a long, wavering way, terribly rough in some places for Brownie, but cheery for me, for Big Trees were seldom out of sight. We crossed the rugged, picturesque basins of Redwood Creek, the North Fork of the Kaweah, and Marble Fork gloriously forested, and full of beautiful cascades and falls, sheer and slanting, infinitely varied with broad curly foam fleeces and strips of embroidery in which the sunbeams revel. Thence we climbed into the noble forest on the Marble and Middle Fork Divide. After a general exploration of the Kaweah basin, this park of the sequoia belt seemed to me the finest, and I then named it 'the Giant Forest.' It extends, a magnificent growth of giants grouped in pure temple groves, ranged in colonnades along the sides of meadows, or scattered among the other trees, from the granite headlands overlooking the hot foothills and plains of the San Joaquin back to within a few miles of the old glacier fountains at an elevation of five thousand to eighty-four hundred feet above the sea.

"When I entered the sublime wilderness the day was nearly done, the trees with rosy, glowing countenances seemed to be hushed and thoughtful, as if waiting in conscious religious dependence on the sun, and one naturally walked softly and awestricken among them. I wandered on, meeting nobler trees where all are noble, subdued in the general calm, as if in some vast hall pervaded by the deepest sanctities and solemnities that sway human souls. At sundown the trees seemed to cease their worship and breathe free. I heard the birds going home. . . . Then I took a walk up the meadow to see the trees in the pale light. They seemed still more marvelously massive and tall than by day, heaving their colossal heads into the depths of the sky, among

[152]

FURNACE CREEK INN, DEATH VALLEY

Photographs—Department of the Interior
Courtesy—Portfolio, American Planning and Civic Association

THE SUN-SCORCHED SANDS OF DEATH VALLEY

ARRIVING AT GLACIER NATIONAL PARK BY TRAIN, VISITORS MAY SOON FIND
THEMSELVES ON PICTURESQUE AND INSPIRING TRAILS

BOULDER PASS IN GLACIER NATIONAL PARK

Photographs—Department of the Interior   Courtesy—Portfolio, American Planning and Civic Association

the stars, some of which appeared to be sparkling on their branches like flowers."

In the Giant Forest is General Sherman Tree, probably the biggest living *Sequoia gigantea* in the world, though remnants and snags in the redwood forests indicate that there have been larger trees. The bole of General Sherman is fluted symmetrically and tapers so little that it might be considered a column of perfection in some giant edifice which would rival the Parthenon. The crown shows clearly the shaping described by John Muir as characteristic of the old Big Trees. In the book on the "Big Trees," by Judge Fry and Colonel White, the bark of General Sherman is described: "Generally of a rich cinnamon brown, it has a reddish tinge that is accentuated at sunset. In places the bark is deeply fluted or furrowed up and down the tree; in spots it seems fuzzy or furry. But you will also note running the length of the tree, up to the first large branches and even higher, long streaks of bark that are shiny or silvered in comparison with areas near by. On most old Big Trees you will see these silvery streaks of bark, and they are usually a sign that centuries, perhaps a score of centuries, ago a mighty fire raged up the tree, almost devouring it. Using sequoia measures of time, centuries instead of days or weeks or years, that is *new* bark. It covers great areas of the trees that have been burned."

But it is not General Sherman alone, or even the amount of timber which the Big Tree would yield, that makes us stand spellbound in contemplation of the age-old forces which have produced such a tree. There is an impressiveness and beauty in the redwood forests that could not be captured by any single tree. No other trees better picture the phrase "forest aisles" than the stately columns of the Big Trees rising straight to heaven. It is an experience to walk between these warm brown pillars, where only occasional glimpses of the sky may be discovered. The forest floor is especially beautiful. Again quoting John Muir: "Under the huge trees up come the small plant people, putting forth fresh leaves and blossoming in such profusion that the hills and valleys would still seem gloriously rich and glad were all the grand trees away. By the side of melting snowbanks rise the crimson sarcodes, round topped and massive as the sequoias themselves, and beds of blue violets and larger yellow ones with leaves curiously lobed; azalea and saxifrage, daisies and lilies on the mossy banks of the streams; and a little way back of them, beneath the trees and on sunny spots on the hills around the groves, wild rose and rubus, spiraea and ribes, mitella, tiarella, campanula, monardella, forget-me-not, and many of them as worthy of lore immortality as the famous Scotch daisy, wanting only a Burns to sing them home to all hearts. . . .

"Imbedded in these majestic woods there are numerous meadows, around the sides of which the Big Trees press close together in beautiful lines, showing their grandeur openly from the ground to their domed heads in the sky. . . . For every venerable lightning-stricken tree, there is one or more in the glory of prime, and for each of these, many young trees and crowds of saplings. The young trees express the grandeur of their race in a way indefinable by any words at my command. When they are five or six feet in diameter and a hundred and fifty feet high, they seem like mere baby saplings as many inches in diameter, their juvenile habit and gestures completely veiling their real size, even to those who, from long experience, are able to make fair approximation in their measurements of common trees."

The life history of these Big Tree forests runs from seedlings to giants around four thousand years old. These ancients are not lone survivors of a past age; they stand in living communities amid trees of their kind of all ages. It was to preserve incomparable groves that Sequoia National Park was created.

General Grant National Park, comprising about four square miles, preserves another extensive grove, and can be reached from Sequoia by the spectacular Generals Highway. General Grant Tree is the largest redwood in the Grant Grove, and while it is said that it would not furnish quite as much lumber as General Sherman, a tree with a forty-foot diameter at the base, which is 267 feet high (matching a twenty-seven-story skyscraper) certainly must command our admiration. General Grant, which has a beauty of form and posture all its own, has sometimes been called the Nation's Christmas tree. Certainly when snow lies in soft puffs on its branches, the surrounding forest of lesser trees furnishing a frame of white etched in on the dark green of the conifers and the darker browns, grays, and blacks of the boles, one could accept the symbol and be thankful that a beneficent Government had pledged its honor to protect these Giants.

Sequoia National Park, with the 352 square miles added in 1926, now is a park 604 miles square and contains the highest mountain peak in the continental United States—Mt. Whitney —and the southern climax of the High Sierra. Of the sixty peaks in the United States which are over 14,000 feet high, thirteen are in California and six in the Sequoia National Park. The park offers fine opportunities for pack-train trips both within and without the park. Many of the Kings Canyon pack trips start from Lodge Pole, the end of the road running north from Giant Forest, passing over J. O. Pass and on into the South Fork of the Kings. But the trip *par excellence* is the trip up Mt. Whitney, across the Kern Canyon. If the marvelously picturesque country is to be seen and enjoyed to the full, at least two weeks is needed—a most interesting and enjoyable two weeks!

Walter A. Starr, Jr., in the "Guide to the John Muir Trail and the High Sierra Region," has commented on the park: "The Sequoia National Park region includes the headwaters of the Kern and Kaweah Rivers, separated by the Great Western Divide, which extends north and south, parallel to the Sierra Crest about midway across the park. Between the Sierra Crest and this great divide the Kern flows south. On the western slope of the divide the various forks of the Kaweah take their rise and flow westward, meeting just west of the park at Three Rivers to form the main stream. Scattered over the extensive basin of the Kaweah, in the western half of the park, are twenty-two groves of giant sequoias. . . . From Foresters Pass on the northern boundary of Sequoia National Park, the Muir Trail crosses the high plateau of the Kern to the summit of Mount Whitney. The last part of the route, from Wallace Creek is along the new High Sierra Trail from Whitney to Giant Forest. . . . Foresters Pass is the highest pass on the Muir Trail. The view north, extending to the Palisades and beyond, is one of the finest views from any pass in the Sierra, and is comparable to that from Junction Pass a mile to the east. By ascending Junction Peak. . . a short distance to the East, a panorama even more remarkable is presented, for this peak occupies a strategic position at the juncture of the Sierra Crest and the Kings-Kern Divide, offering an unobstructed sweep in all directions. The view southward along the Sierra Crest includes the Whitney group of 14,000-foot peaks—the end of the grand crescendo of the Sierra."

Hardy mountaineers who desire to test their skill and command the world from the clouds may find peaks aplenty to climb. Sequoia National Park, with the highest mountain and the biggest tree, cannot fail to capture and hold the attention of the American people. There are excellent accommodations at Giant Forest Lodge and public campgrounds at Giant Forest, Lodge Pole, and Dorst Creek. The camp-sites are laid out according to modern standards and, somewhat removed from the highway, provide idyllic conditions for camping. Sequoia National Park is a place where one may penetrate the wilderness and sleep out under the sky, for in the dry season there is little or no rain.

Sequoia is open the year round, and in winter there are fine opportunities for skiing, tobogganing, and snowshoeing. In summer there is also a daily bear feed. The campfire programs are well attended throughout the summer and are educational as well as inspiring. Colonel John R. White, who served the park as superintendent from 1920 to 1939, deserves the congratulations of the American people for the increasing protection which is being given to the Big Trees and for the atmosphere of reverence which he has created in the park.

MONUMENTS

In California there are eight national monuments (including the Channel Islands), covering 2,802,300 acres, of which the largest and most unique is Death Valley, established as a monument in 1933 and now containing 1,907,720 acres. Once a death trap for the pioneers who sought to cross the sun-scorched sands, it is now a favorite tourist resort, where one can see a great desert bowl nearly 300 feet below the level of the sea, and raise one's eyes to Telescope Peak which pierces the clouds at 11,325 feet in altitude. The Park Service has called attention to the "pastel colors of the rocks, intricately carved and bare of vegetation, the browns and hazy purple masses of the distant mountains, the wide, white expanses of salt and alkali, the sweeping curves of sand dunes."

MANY GLACIER HOTEL

GLACIER
NATIONAL PARK

GOING-TO-THE-SUN CHALET

Photographs—Department of the Interior

Courtesy—Portfolio, American Planning
and Civic Association

Photograph—Department of the Interior   Courtesy—American Planning and Civic Annual

KINNERLY PEAK, FROM KINTLA LAKE,
GLACIER NATIONAL PARK

THE MAGIC ROCKIES

The Rocky Mountain parks deserve a separate and special trip if they are to be seen and appreciated, although, of course, it is possible for those who live in the East to stop over in Glacier and Yellowstone on the way to the Northwest and in Rocky Mountain National Park on the way to California or the Southwest. However, the ideal tour would be to start at Glacier National Park on the Canadian border and then to visit Yellowstone, the Tetons, and Rocky Mountain National Park, staying long enough in each to learn something about it. One might even say that three summer vacations could well be given to Glacier, to Yellowstone and the Tetons, and to Rocky Mountain Park.

GLACIER NATIONAL PARK

Except for Yellowstone and Mt. McKinley, Glacier National Park is the largest in the system. Its 1,534 square miles in northwestern Montana include some of the most spectacular mountain crests and peaks in America, spotted with half a hundred glaciers and two hundred glistening lakes. It adjoins the Waterton Lakes Park in Canada, and the two by Presidential proclamation, authorized by Congress and the Canadian Government, form the Waterton-Glacier International Peace Park.

Glacier National Park is readily accessible by train to the eastern entrance to the park, a thousand miles west of St. Paul and a little over six hundred east of Seattle, and by airplane to nearby cities. It is by automobile that our imaginary trip will enter the park from the east, stopping first, if desired, at Glacier Park Hotel, adjacent to the railroad station, but preferably for fishermen or hikers going direct to Two Medicine Lake where, either at Two Medicine Chalet or the public camp, the setting sun may be seen across the mountain-bound lake in which the massive slopes of snow-patched Sinopah are reflected in rose, gray, and white. A boat trip across the lake may be taken to the foot of Mt. Sinopah. Almost everyone takes the easy forest path to Twin Falls. There is excellent fishing in the lake and in the streams. The evening campfires at Two Medicine, conducted by the ranger naturalists, have always been popular; they

[161]

cap a day's hiking or fishing with just that relaxation which permits attention to a talk explaining or commenting on what has been seen during the day.

Trick Falls, near the highway bridge, on the Two Medicine Road, is so easily accessible that perhaps it is not given its full rating of beauty, as hikers are apt to value the beauty of scenic features by the effort exerted to reach them.

Practically everyone who goes to Glacier makes a visit to Many Glacier Hotel or to the nearby camp, by way of the dead-end access road into the east-central part of the park. The self-guided walks around Lake Josephine toward Grinnell Glacier are entertaining and easy, and even easier are the boat trips on Lake Josephine and Swiftcurrent Lakes.

In the old days, visitors drove to the head of St. Mary Lake and there took a boat to Going-to-the-Sun, one of the most beautiful and secluded spots in the park. Nothing can destroy the fine combination of snow-etched mountains and sparkling lake, but since the Going-to-the-Sun Highway skirts the lake and brings thousands of automobiles to rest on the leveled-off parking space back of the Chalet, much of the romance and wildness of this once-enchanted spot have been dissipated.

Going-to-the-Sun Highway runs from St. Mary, past Going-to-the-Sun, over Logan Pass, to skirt Lake McDonald to Belton, where the superintendent's office is located. It cannot be denied that the drive is very scenic and that it introduces the heart of the park to the automobile visitor. North and south of this highway are great areas reached only by trail.

When the weather is clear and the views are not obscured by rain and clouds, the trip up the east side of the park, partly outside the boundaries, to Waterton Lakes, is very worthwhile and brings visitors into the Canadian Rockies. Just outside the boundary on the west side of the park is a Forest Service road which gives access to many trails—one, in the extreme north-western section of the park along the Kintla Lakes to the foot of Waterton Lake. A road to the foot of Bowman Lake connects with a lakeside trail finally joining the Kintla Lake trail.

One could spend weeks and months in traveling the trails of Glacier National Park. There are many shelter cabins scattered over the park for the comfort and convenience of the hiker, in addition to the many public camps, hotels, and chalets for both hiker and motorist.

The National Park Service has called attention to the geography of Glacier: "Glacier Park has within its boundary two parallel mountain ranges. The eastern, or front range, extends from the Canadian boundary almost without a break to New Mexico. The western, or Livingston Range, rises at the head of Lake McDonald, becomes the front range beyond the international line, and runs northward to Alaska. Between these two ranges in the center of the park is a broad swell which carries the Continental Divide from one to the other. This is Flattop Mountain, whose groves of trees are open and parklike, wholly unlike the dense forests of the lowlands. . . . A trail leads from Waterton over Flattop to the tent camp, called Fifty Mountain, and to Granite Park, where a comfortable high-mountain chalet is located. Here is exposed a great mass of lava, which once welled up from the interior of the earth and spread over the region which was then the bottom of a sea. The chalets command a fine view of the majestic grouping of mountains around Logan Pass, of the noble summits of the Livingston Range, and of systems far to the south and west of the park. Extending in the near foreground are gentle slopes covered with sparse clumps of stunted vegetation. In early July open spaces are gold-carpeted with glacier lilies and bizarrely streaked with lingering snow patches. Beyond are the deep, heavy forests of Upper McDonald Valley."

From these chalets, too, there is a foot trail to the rim of the Garden Wall, where may be seen the "heavenly blue alpine columbine" together with many others, including dryads, globe flowers, and alpine fireweed.

The mere catalogue of trails and trips in Glacier Park would require pages. Since the time when the late George Bird Grinnell made his first trip to Glacier in 1885, later to be publicized in an article in *Century Magazine*, the park has been a magnet for true lovers of mountains and mountain trips. There are extensive wilderness areas in the park, far from roads of any kind, where only hardy hikers and pack trains may penetrate. Of Glacier it may well be said: "So much to see, so much to learn, so much to enjoy!"

[163]

YELLOWSTONE NATIONAL PARK

The immutables of Yellowstone are today much the same as they were in the seventies when the early exploring trips revealed the marvels of the region. Nearly forty years ago John Muir said of the Yellowstone: "It is a big, wholesome wilderness on the broad summit of the Rocky Mountains, favored with abundance of rain and snow,—a place of fountains where the greatest of the American rivers take their rise. The central portion is a densely forested and comparatively level volcanic plateau with an average elevation of about eight thousand feet above the sea, surrounded by an imposing host of mountains belonging to the subordinate Gallatin, Wind River, Teton, Absaroka, and snowy ranges. Unnumbered lakes shine in it, united by a famous band of streams that rush up out of hot lava beds, or fall from the frosty peaks in channels rocky and bare, mossy and bosky to the main rivers, singing cheerily on through every difficulty, cunningly dividing and finding their way to the two far-off seas.

"Glacier meadows and beaver meadows are outspread with charming effect along the banks of the streams, parklike expanses in the woods, and innumerable small gardens in rocky recesses of the mountains, some of them containing more petals than leaves, while the whole wilderness is enlivened with happy animals.

"Beside the treasures common to most mountain regions that are wild and blessed with a kind climate, the park is full of exciting wonders. The wildest geysers in the world, in bright, triumphant bands, are dancing and singing in it amid thousands of boiling springs, beautiful and awful, their basins arrayed in gorgeous colors like gigantic flowers; and hot paint-pots, mud springs, mud volcanoes, mush and broth caldrons whose contents are of every color and consistency, plash and heave and roar in bewildering abundance. In the adjacent mountains, beneath the living trees the edges of petrified forests are exposed to view, like specimens on the shelves of a museum, standing on ledges tier above tier where they grew, solemnly silent in rigid crystalline beauty after swaying in the winds thousands of centuries ago, opening marvelous views back into the years and climates and life of the past. Here, too, are hills of sparkling crystals, hills of sulphur, hills of glass, hills of cinders and ashes,

THE SIERRA CLUB VISITS GRINNELL LAKE

GLACIER NATIONAL PARK

BOWMAN LAKE

Photographs—Charles S. Webber   Courtesy—Sierra Club Bulletin

MOUNTAIN GOATS IN GLACIER NATIONAL PARK

mountains of every style of architecture, icy or forested, mountains covered with honey-bloom sweet as Hymettus, mountains boiled soft like potatoes and colored like a sunset sky."

All these wonders are there today. Yellowstone Lake still reflects the woods and mountains and sky. The two magnificent falls of the Grand Canyon of the Yellowstone still splash the waters of the river over the highly colored stones which gave name to the lake and river. Moran's pictures are as truly photographic today as when they were painted.

Yellowstone has four principal entrances which connect with a double-loop road. The drives in themselves are charming and interesting. With "Haynes Guide" and "Trailside Notes for the Motorist and Hiker," covering Mammoth to Old Faithful and Fishing Bridge Museum to Mammoth, one can drive to all the principal points of interest and see understandingly the sights of Yellowstone. There are 328 miles of roads in the 3,437 square miles of the park, and 920 miles of trails. The road mileage has not been increased in the last thirty years, but old dirt roads have been improved with hard surface and sometimes relocated in the interests of safety. One could hardly imagine a more fascinating game than to make leisurely trips around Yellowstone to examine the 3,000 geysers and hot springs at different times of day. There are guided trips from all centers both for automobiles and on foot. There are campfire programs at many places in the park. There are a number of most illuminating museums. And Yellowstone has a bear show in which the grizzly gentry come out to feed, and which attracts a great deal of attention. There are miles of good fishing, hiking, and riding.

The season at Yellowstone is short, for in winter the park lies under a deep mantle of snow and the temperatures reach incredibly low levels. There are hotels, lodges, and public camps at Mammoth Hot Springs, Old Faithful, the Lake, and the Canyon. In spite of the large number of visitors accommodated in the popular centers, amounting at the height of the season, with park and hotel staffs, to veritable towns, it is possible to see the marvels of the park without *feeling* overcome with the crowds. And there is still much wilderness in the park which it is hoped will never be invaded with roads and hotels and lodges. Every citizen of the United States may be thankful for Yellowstone.

THE GRAND TETON NATIONAL PARK

Those same Grand Tetons which were landmarks to the pioneers who crossed the continent in the early days, now rear their craggy crests in a spectacular jagged silhouette against the sky. For many years efforts were made to enlarge Yellowstone National Park to include the Tetons, historic Jackson Hole, and the Absarokas. But, as in most other projects to increase the national parks, the resistance on the part of those who desired to make use of the resources has been very great. It was not until 1929 that a twenty-seven-mile strip, from three to nine miles wide, was created a national park. This took in the eastern slopes of the entire range of Tetons from their ragged crests to the string of crystal lakes which gird them at the base of the steep slopes. It is well recognized by park-minded conservationists that every area worthy of being a national park should have a sufficiently wide protective rim to preserve the character of its scenery. It was soon apparent to close observers that the uncontrolled areas adjoining the park were becoming a menace to its use as a park. Along the county road, on private property in Jackson Hole, there grew up the most unsightly structures, and many of these were put to noisy uses totally incompatible with the enjoyment of a national park. Mr. John D. Rockefeller, Jr., observed this when he made a visit to the Grand Teton National Park, and he purchased some 40,000 acres of private property which, with available public domain and some national-forest land, it has been proposed to add to the Teton Park as a permanent protection, but so far selfish local interests have prevented action by Congress to accept the gift and make the transfers. The Jackson Hole country which would thus be added to the park has an interesting history of its own. In the thirties and forties many famous pioneers were identified with Jackson Hole—Captain Bonneville, Father De Smet, Rev. Samuel Parker, Jedediah Smith, Jim Bridger, Kit Carson, David Jackson, Captain William Sublette, Joe Meek, and others. There has been a sprinkling of dude ranches in and around Jackson Hole of recent years, and some of these are still operated on land which Mr. Rockefeller purchased.

One complication which no way has been found to remove is that Jackson Lake, once a part of the crystal string of gems,

FISHING BRIDGE MUSEUM, YELLOWSTONE NATIONAL PARK

YELLOWSTONE FALLS

Photographs—Department of the Interior
Courtesy—Portfolio, American Planning and Civic Association

Photograph—Beckett Howorth   Courtesy—Appalachia.

THE GRAND TETON

[170]

THE GRAND TETONS, WITH JACKSON HOLE FOREGROUND WHICH JOHN D. ROCKEFELLER, JR.
HAS PURCHASED TO GIVE TO THE FEDERAL GOVERNMENT, TO BE ADDED TO
THE GRAND TETON NATIONAL PARK

TEEWINOT AND JACKSON HOLE, FROM THE GRAND TETON

DREAM LAKE, ROCKY MOUNTAIN NATIONAL PARK

[172]

was terribly damaged some years ago by what is now believed to have been an unjustified reclamation project. The level of the lake was raised without even the precaution of taking out the dead timber, so that those who had loved the lake in early days came back to see the tragedy of its ruin. In recent years, CCC crews have cleared out the dead timber, but the dam and the ugly changes in the level of the lake still mar the scenery of the park. Since there are other storage sites lower down which could give to Idaho the same and more water, it is devoutly to be hoped that a way may be found to redeem the lake.

The Grand Tetons offer excellent mountain-climbing opportunities. The trails are used by both hikers and horsemen, for Jackson Hole is still a center for western saddle horses. There is an excellent museum, and the campfire lectures on the geology of the region are attended by those who come from a wide radius. When the protective additions are made, the Grand Teton National Park will become one of the finest of the national parks.

ROCKY MOUNTAIN NATIONAL PARK

The Colorado Rockies have long ranked high in the affections of the American people. There are some of the highest and finest peaks in the entire range in the Rocky Mountain Park. Longs Peak, the tallest, reaches 14,255 feet. The Trail Ridge Road, which crosses the Continental Divide, connects the town of Estes Park on the east side of the park with Grand Lake on the west side, and gives to the motorist some of the finest mountain views in America. According to the national park bulletin, a distinguishing feature of the park is its "profusion of precipice-walled canyons lying between lofty mountains." We are told that "Ice-cold streams wander from lake to lake, watering wild flowers of luxuriance and beauty. The entire park is a garden of wild flowers. . . . There are few wilder and lovelier spots . . . than Loch Vale, 3,000 feet sheer below Taylor Peak. Adjoining it lies Glacier Gorge on the precipitous western slope of Longs Peak and enclosing a group of small lakes. These, with lesser gorges cradling Bear Lake, picturesque Dream Lake, beautiful Fern Lake, and exquisite Odessa Lake, and still others yet unnamed, constitute the wild gardens of the Rocky Mountain National Park, lying in the angle north of Longs Peak; while in the angle south lies a little-known wilderness of lakes and gorges called Wild Basin.''

And yet Rocky Mountain National Park, which has so much to make it one of the great parks of the system, has been a sort of stepchild from the beginning. The boundaries were drawn far too closely when it was created in 1915. Rocky Mountain was one of the parks to which the Reclamation Service was given free entry. There was a diversion ditch in the north end of the park which it was legal to extend, and extended it was a few years ago, so that all who ride over the Trail Ridge Road see now the long gash scar of this unsightly intrusion. Grand Lake, which once was the largest and most picturesque body of water in the region, was not included in the park, and although under authorization of Congress, purchase of some of the lands along its border has been progressing, private occupation has quite transformed its once wild beauty. There are many private holdings well within its boundaries, so that it is utterly impossible to give protection to great areas which are scenically a part of the park. And then, to cap the long history of misfortunes which have been visited on it, Congress authorized in 1938 the building of a water-diversion tunnel under the park which will affect the surroundings of Grand Lake, will involve a ditch in an authorized addition to the park, and introduce power lines and plants along the picturesque Thompson-River approach to the park. Technically, if the assurance of the Reclamation Service that no air shafts will have to be sunk inside of the park can be realized, there will be no entry into the existing park; but no one who is familiar with the surroundings can escape the conviction that areas which should have been included in the park will be injured. There is an extensive region south of the park where are some fine peaks, glaciers, and lakes which might well be added to the present boundaries.

There are five public campgrounds in the park and many hotels, lodges, and camps on private lands in or near it. It is to be hoped that the private holdings in the Rocky Mountain Park will soon be acquired and that old injuries will be allowed to heal wherever possible.

OVER THE SEAS

It seems logical to include the trips to the over-seas national parks under the section on western parks, as most of those who visit Alaska and Hawaii sail from western ports.

MT. MCKINLEY

Regular steamers ply between Seattle and Alaska ports, giving passengers one of the most picturesque coastwise ocean trips imaginable. Once arrived in Alaska, there is a rail trip of 348 miles from Seward to McKinley Park Station. According to the national park bulletin, the trip to the park from Seward "takes the passenger past beautiful Lake Kenai, Moose Pass, Spencer Glacier, and Turnagain Arm, which boasts the second highest tide in the world. It also offers the unique experience of crossing the Continental Divide at its lowest point in North America, where it reaches 2,337 feet elevation. The first view of Mt. McKinley is had from Talkeetna, but the majestic peak is sighted from various other points along the railroad."

Next to Yellowstone, Mt. McKinley is the largest of our national parks and in it lies the highest of North American mountains, its great white expanse at the highest point reaching 20,300 feet. Its sculpturing is in simple broad planes of shining white ice and snow which cover the mighty mountain two-thirds of the way down from its summit, which is 17,000 feet above the plateau on the north and west. Mt. Foraker, near by, is 17,000 feet high; other peaks are somewhat lower but impressive because of the distance above the "take-off." Both McKinley and Foraker have been climbed in recent years.

The Alaska glaciers offer a fine opportunity for study, and both for the scientist and the layman the wildlife of the park is fascinating. Caribou, moose, Toklat grizzly bears, Alaska mountain sheep, wolves, wolverines, coyotes, Alaska red fox, hoary marmots, lynx, beaver, martens and minks, land otters, Mackenzie snowshoe rabbits, Alaska conies, ground squirrels, short-billed gulls, the coy Alaska willow ptarmigan, and surf-birds are all found.

Within the park there are eighty miles of graveled motor roads, and there are excellent saddle-horse trails which lead to the regions about the base of Mt. McKinley and to other points of interest. Unless one is an experienced mountain climber and a part of an organized expedition, the best way to see Mt. McKinley is from the air. Hotel and tent camps are available.

Those who covet wilderness may certainly find it in Mt. McKinley National Park. The trip to Alaska, the visit to the park, with side trips to Glacier Bay National Monument of over a million acres, reached from Juneau by boat, and Katmai National Monument of two and a half million acres, reached by sailing vessel from Kodiak, is guaranteed to satisfy hunger for the back country.

HAWAII

Honolulu, the capital of the Territory of Hawaii, is reached in a four-and-a-half- to six-day ocean voyage from San Francisco or Los Angeles. Honolulu is also a port of call of steamers from the Orient, Australia, and Vancouver, B. C. The Hawaii National Park is in two sections, one including the active craters of Mauna Loa and Kilauea, covering 219 square miles of the Island of Hawaii, where the Port of Hilo is reached by Inter-Island steamers or Inter-Island airplanes from Honolulu. The other section covers the dormant crater of Haleakala on the Island of Maui.

The contrast between glacier-bound Alaska, with its national park open during a short summer season, and the Hawaiian Islands, lying just south of the Tropic of Cancer, with their everlasting summer and lush tropical verdure, is very great.

Kilauea, perhaps older than the much higher Mauna Loa, creates the impression of being a crater in the side of the larger mountain. From Hilo there is an excellent highway to the Volcano House, on the northeast rim overlooking the entire crater of Kilauea, roughly four miles in diameter. The trail from the Volcano House across this expanse of purgatorial desolation, cut by many steam cracks from which hot vapor pours forth, is an introduction to the deep pit of Halemaumau, about half a mile in diameter. Sometimes this pit is sunken a thousand feet or more and sometimes the molten lava boils up to its very surface, a lake of living fire. At night, then, the steam and heat

BIGHORNS IN ROCKY MOUNTAIN NATIONAL PARK

Photograph—Department of the Interior   Courtesy—Portfolio, American Planning and Civic Association

THE JOY OF A PACK-TRAIN TRIP

Photograph—Department of the Interior   ELEVATION 20,300 FEET   Courtesy—Sierra Club Bulletin

MT. McKINLEY, THE HIGHEST PEAK
IN NORTH AMERICA

Photograph—K. Maehara

THE 1924 KILAUEA ERUPTION
IN HAWAII NATIONAL PARK

take on a fiery aspect. In some of the great eruptions, as in 1934, "without much preliminary warning, molten lava again returned to the fire pit in Kilauea. This eruption in its early stages was one of the most spectacular on record. Highly charged with gas released from the tremendous pressure, the frothy lava burst through a crack 700 feet long, halfway up the western wall of the crater, cascading in rivers of fire 425 feet to the floor below. The force of the lava cracked open the old floor left by the 1931–32 eruption across its northern and northwest end, and along the foot of the western wall dense clouds of sulphur fumes poured out, as the fiery fountains shot the liquid lava high into the air. As in the previous eruption, blocks of light pumice thrown out from the vents were whirled upward by the heat currents and gales of wind and deposited in shattered fragments over the land for more than a mile to leeward. In a few days the crater had been filled with new lava to a depth of 70 feet, and instead of the countless frothy fountains of the initial outbreak the activity centered in a lake of fire with from 5 to 10 fountains throwing jets of lava from 50 to 200 feet above the lake."

There are thirty-nine miles of highway within the Kilauea area. There are also trails which make possible a three- or four-day riding or hiking trip to the summit crater of Mauna Loa, the round trip covering about fifty miles. Mauna Loa rises to a height of 13,680 feet above the floor of the surrounding Pacific Ocean. The writer once traveled from Honolulu to see a vast flow from Mauna Loa, which came thirty miles, to the edge of the ocean. The flow was about half a mile wide, and by the time it reached the strand along the sea, it was moving very slowly. At night, as the steamer approached, a glow could be seen in the sky, and at intervals the living trees, overtaken by the great glowing embers, would burst into flames. It was necessary to walk across a stretch of "aa"—hard, flinty cinders which resulted from thin, hot molten lava.

When those who had traveled from Honolulu to see the great spectacle came close to the face of the flow, it presented at times a gray, ashy and cinder effect, like a great banked furnace. At first the movement was not perceptible, but soon it was seen that every little while the clinkers would stir, and, as though some great giant were poking the fire, great embers as large as a house would break away from the mass, split open to show a red-hot surface, and then gradually gray over again like a dying fire. It was uncanny to see koa and other trees with bright green leaves pushed by the inexorable coals, shrivel and die in the course of a very few minutes, and as the fire grew hotter, finally burst into flames and disappear altogether.

There have been eruptions from Mauna Loa many times. According to the bulletin of the National Park Service: "Following a rather violent earthquake which occurred at 1:11 a.m., November 21, 1935, and was felt generally over the entire island of Hawaii, and on Maui and Oaho as well, Mauna Loa erupted at 7:35 p.m. in its northern summit crater. . . . The flow of lava. . . was notable in that it produced both the aa and pahoehoe types of lava. The activity continued until January 2, 1936, when forward motion of the flow ceased at a point near the headwaters of the Wailuku River, about 18 miles from the city of Hilo. . . . On December 27 a squadron of United States Army planes dropped 6 tons of TNT near the point of emergence of the lava stream." The flow almost immediately slowed down.

One of the always surprising manifestations comes from the many steam cracks which emit hot vapor in the green-covered areas. The drives and trails traverse the most charming tropical forests, their floors covered with dense forests of tree ferns. The trees, flowers, and fruits comprise many not familiar to those who live in temperate zones.

The stop-over on Maui or the special trip to Haleakala brings to view a mountain a little over 10,000 feet high, once much higher, but with a great crater 7½ miles long by 3 miles wide, with walls over 1,000 feet high. Within these colored walls "lies a superb spectacle. Covering the floor are giant red, black, and orange cinder cones which, though hundreds of feet high, are dwarfed by the immensity of their surroundings."

Thus, both the extinct and the active volcanoes are great sights. And the by-product of the Hawaiian scene, with the tropical life of plants, animals, and people, and the contact with the old Hawaiian traditions, is an added lure which draws many tourists from the mainland to this island territory.

THE OLD SOUTHWEST

GRAND CANYON

OUR journey in the Old Southwest will begin at Grand Canyon, reached easily by rail and highway from east and west. It is quite sure that the reactions of those who stand today on the South Rim and look at the great spectacle are far different from the emotions of that little band of Spanish soldiers who, led by Don Lopez de Cardenas in 1540, met with such keen disappointment when they realized that no gold was to be found there—only a view!

In 1896, when John Muir visited the Canyon, he wrote in his journal: "At 6:15 p. m. I ran up to the verge of the Canyon and had my first memorable and overwhelming view in the light and shade of the setting sun. It is the most tremendous expression of erosion and the most ornate and complicated I ever saw. Man seeks the finest marbles for sculptures; Nature takes cinders, ashes, sediments, and makes all divine in fineness of beauty—turrets, towers, pyramids, battlemented castles, rising in glowing beauty from the depths of this canyon of canyons noiselessly hewn from the smooth mass of the featureless plateau." He thought the storm "dimmed. . . with the silken brush of the rain" the wondrous structure. Later he wrote: "It seems a gigantic statement, for even Nature to make, all in one mighty stone word. Wildness so Godful, cosmic, primeval, bestows a new sense of earth's beauty and size. . . . But the colors, the living, rejoicing colors, chanting, morning and evening, in chorus to heaven! Whose brush or pencil, however lovingly inspired, can give us these?"

The first Government exploration party to go into the region was under the leadership of Lieutenant Ives of the War Department, who in 1858 traveled by steamboat up the Colorado River to Black Canyon, in which Boulder Dam is now located. In 1869–71, Major J. W. Powell traveled with rowboats down the Colorado River. His studies gave the reading world the first scientific descriptions of the geological formation of the canyon walls.

The workaday explanation of the beauty of the Grand Canyon lies in erosion. The Colorado River contributed its share, working away many an eon, and the winds and the rain and the plant life joined in to produce a picture such as can be seen nowhere else in the world. Of course there was a long geological history before this last chapter. The Archean Age is represented by the crystalline schists, gneisses, and granites at the bottom of the Canyon. Summarizing the scientific account presented in that charming book on the "Grand Canyon Country," by M. R. Tillotson, so many years superintendent of the park, and Frank J. Taylor, it is recorded that the surface of these rocks, after they had been subjected to such great heat and internal pressure that many were in nearly vertical positions, which later eroded to a plain, was submerged with the water and sediments of the Algonkian era. After the deposits came to be some 12,000 feet in thickness, there was an extensive uplifting of the earth's crust, tilting the rocks above the surface of the ocean in which they were laid. After erosion had produced a rolling plain there came a second submergence, and the Cambrian Age had been reached. The succeeding geological ages left little writing to read, but in the early Carboniferous Age there was a third submergence, during which was deposited the calcium carbonate now represented by the 500 vertical feet of red-wall limestone of the Mississippian Age. Then came the Permian Age which left some of the most primitive reptilian tracks, and the Coconino sandstones. Then followed the fourth and long-continued submergence, and from this we have the Kaibab limestone, the topmost stratum of the Canyon walls, though it is estimated that there was once a deposit of 6,000 or 7,000 feet on top of the limestone. This particular stone page may be read at Cedar Mountain, two miles from Desert View. In the Vermillion Cliffs and in Zion and Bryce, complete successions of these and younger formations may be seen. The erosion which removed this overlay required many millions of years. And then the Colorado River flowed into the scene, and with its burden of sediment and loose gravel as cutting tools, it has hewn for us this great Grand Canyon.

The National Park overlooks the Canyon. From the South Rim, which is some 7,000 feet in altitude, there are hundreds of marvelous lookouts along the fifty miles of rim drives. This part of the park is open the year round. Excellent accommodations may be had at El Tovar, built in 1904, at Bright Angel Lodge

THE GRAND CANYON OF THE COLORADO

Photographs—Department of the Interior   Courtesy—Portfolio, American Planning and Civic Association

EL TOVAR HOTEL, GRAND CANYON

BRIGHT ANGEL LODGE ON SOUTH RIM OF GRAND CANYON

Photographs—Department of the Interior   Courtesy—Portfolio, American Planning and Civic Association

LUXURIOUS CABINS ON NORTH RIM OF GRAND CANYON

Photograph—Department of the Interior   Courtesy—Portfolio, American Planning and Civic Association

THE GREAT WHITE THRONE, ZION NATIONAL PARK

BRYCE CANYON NATIONAL PARK

and cabins, rebuilt in recent years, and at the public camp in the pleasant forest.

The Grand Canyon opens up an entirely new world. Every visitor should read the Tillotson and Taylor book on the ground. The Park Service issues two interesting Guide Leaflets, which should be in the hands of everyone who takes the Desert View Drive and the West Rim Drive. These, with the regular park bulletin, and such other books as may be selected from the bibliography, add greatly to the understanding of the Canyon. There is an observation station at Yavapai Point, where there is a magnificent view of the Canyon. From the parapet, powerful glasses are trained on some of the most interesting points. Pertinent exhibits in the interior room have been arranged to present an illustrated account of the geological history.

The mule trips on the trails down into the floor of the Canyon are always exciting. Horace M. Albright, in the foreword to the Tillotson and Taylor book, remarked: "I have always felt sorry for the traveler so rushed that he can see the Grand Canyon only from the rim. The descent into the great gorge is one of the real adventures of a lifetime. It is only by such a trip that one may know the Grand Canyon intimately or may appreciate the tremendous scope of this outstanding example of erosion."

The entire population of the Canyon gathers every afternoon to see the Hopi dances in front of Hopi House, built across the road from El Tovar for the display of Hopi arts and crafts. The Navajos make their displays outside of hogans typical of those inhabited by their tribe.

From the South Rim one may fly across the Canyon to the North Rim, one may pack across on the trail, or one may drive by Desert View, across the Navajo Bridge, past the Vermillion Cliffs, and then through the lovely Kaibab Forest to the headquarters on the north side of the Canyon. The Grand Canyon Lodge and the campground offer facilities for living and observation 8,000 feet above the sea, enjoyable only in summer, for here the snow blankets the Canyon all winter.

For breath-taking beauty, for geological demonstration, for contact with surviving local Indians, and for trail trips and motor drives of unparalleled and absorbing interest, the Grand Canyon of the Colorado leads in its class!

ZION AND BRYCE NATIONAL PARKS

From the North Rim of the Grand Canyon, a drive of some 125 miles by way of the spectacularly beautiful Zion-Mt. Carmel Highway brings the traveler to Zion Canyon. This approach reveals through the windows of the highway tunnels the first fine views of the highly colored cliffs flanking the valley.

According to the Park Service bulletin: "A 'Yosemite Valley done in oils' comes close to a description of the principal feature of Zion National Park. This gorgeous valley has about the same dimensions as the famous Yosemite Valley. Extraordinary as are the sandstone forms, the color is what most amazes. The deep red of the Vermillion Cliff is the prevailing tint. Two-thirds of the way up, these marvelous walls and temples are painted gorgeous reds; then, above the reds, they rise in startling white. Sometimes the white is surmounted by a cap of vivid red, remains of another red stratum which once overlay all. The Vermillion Cliff rests upon 350 feet of even a more insistent red, relieved by mauve and purple shale. That in turn rests upon a hundred feet of other variegated strata. Through these successive layers of sands and shales and limestones, the Virgin River has cut its amazing valley. The entrance is between two gigantic stone masses of complicated architectural proportions which are named the West Temple and The Watchman."

But the most impressive of all the remarkable mountains of rock is the Great White Throne which rises sheer from the valley floor to display an ethereal white crown surmounting its royal red base. There is something unreal about this huge red and white stone. It seems not to be made of the same material we are accustomed to find forming the earth's surface.

There are twenty miles of road in the park, introducing visitors to the heart of the Canyon. The trails—some twenty-five miles of them—permit those who desire, to walk far up the valley in company with a ranger naturalist or alone, and to explore a number of the high flanking cliffs.

From Zion one may retrace one's way for a short distance over the Zion-Mt. Carmel Highway and then turn north for Bryce. The Grand Canyon is much more stupendous in size and in the heaviness with which the color is laid on. Bryce, being smaller and easier to bring into the perspective of vision, is more like a delicate miniature, with beautiful but thinner colors. The Grand Canyon seems to be done in oils, Bryce in water colors.

There seems little of remarkable interest as one arrives at the headquarters building. But when one walks to the edge of the abyss, there lies Bryce, like a complicated carved cameo, done in shades of white, pink, and deep rose-reds, or, as the Indians said, "red rocks standing like men in a bowl-shaped canyon."

The trail down into the floor of the Canyon is an easy one, either on foot or on horseback. Cut off from all familiar forms of vegetation, surrounded by architectural masses, with fretted ornamentation almost Byzantine in its elaborate sculpturing, one could imagine here a deserted city of the long-distant past.

Many visitors leave Bryce to drive to Cedar City by a route which permits a detour to Cedar Breaks National Monument, another brilliant splash of color. The highway to Cedar City drops down through a rugged canyon by the side of rushing waters and is in itself well worth the trip.

Not very far from Zion and Bryce lies the Escalante, described by Merel Sager as "200 miles of countless, fantastic, weird monuments and pinnacles, slowly yielding to the relentless forces of wind and water." Cut by "the mighty Colorado, mysterious, treacherous, forbidding, carving its meandering way through red sandstone canyons, so rugged that they have thus far successfully defied east and west commutation of human kind in the whole of southeastern Utah," the area is a proposed national monument.

BIG BEND

Big Bend National Park, lying on the border between Texas and Mexico, was authorized to become a national park when the lands shall have been purchased by private and state funds and turned over to the United States Government, free of cost.

Herbert Maier has described the region: "The Big Bend country of Texas is that triangular portion in the southwestern part of the State inclosed by the big bend of the Rio Grande. The romance of the border frontier still lingers in this last wilderness of Texas. No railroad traverses it. Its few roads are largely makeshift, or improvised wagon trails, serving its few ranches and mining claims. The Chisos Mountains range from low, semi-desert slopes to high, wooded canyons and peaks. Between the 3,000- and 8,000-foot elevations are found the Lower and Upper Sonoran Zones, the Transition, and an indication of the Canadian Zone." Then there is the Rio Grande, which "in its tortuous course, cuts through three steep-walled limestone canyons, about 2,000 feet in depth . . . and meanders over the river plains between."

CARLSBAD CAVERNS

In the southeastern part of New Mexico, easily accessible from Texas cities and from the nearby town of Carlsbad, are the most wonderful caverns yet discovered. If they are not colorful canyons, they are certainly colorful caverns. They are so large that it takes hours merely to walk through the principal chambers open to the public. Since the caverns could not be seen in the dark, and since torches could not illumine the distant ceilings, the caverns are equipped with an elaborate system of electric lighting. The extent of the caverns no one yet knows. According to the Park Service bulletin, there are now three main levels, 750 feet, 900 feet, and 1,320 feet underground. It is only to the higher level that visitors are conducted through the seven miles of corridors and chambers. Carlsbad is much visited.

The sculpturing of Carlsbad is as elaborate as that of Bryce or Cedar Breaks, and though not as brilliant, there are yet very lovely colors to be found in the caverns, as in the "Veiled Statue" in the Green Lake Room, or in the gleaming onyx of the walls of the King's Palace. These fanciful names but reflect the sumptuous effect of these great underground chambers.

Geologically, "this (Carlsbad) limestone was formed originally in a shallow inland extension of the ocean some 200 million years ago—in the Permian period, which followed the time of greatest coal forming throughout the world. After this period the area was dry land, but it may have been resubmerged and covered by sediments at a later period.

"The uplifting and folding movements that formed the Rocky Mountains also raised the Carlsbad area above sea level. The Guadalupe Mountains near Carlsbad are outliers of that great

AIR VIEW OF NEEDLES FORMATION, NORTH OF BLUE MOUNTAINS

PROPOSED ESCALANTE NATIONAL MONUMENT, UTAH

GRAND GULCH, RICH IN ARCHEOLOGY, DRAINS INTO THE SAN JUAN RIVER

Courtesy—Portfolio, American Planning and Civic Association

THE BIG BEND COUNTRY (ON THE TEXAS-MEXICAN BOUNDARY, RIO GRANDE
RIVER) WHICH THE GOVERNMENT WILL ACCEPT AS A NATIONAL PARK

mountain system. The uplift of the region took place about the end of the 'Age of Dinosaurs' (Cretaceous period)—60 million years ago.'' Since that time the streams have carved their deep gorges, vast caverns have been hollowed, and within them, still later, the amazing decorative deposits were formed.

MESA VERDE

In southwestern Colorado, reached by highways from Arizona and New Mexico and by rail and highways from Colorado, lies Mesa Verde National Park. Named for the green of the junipers and piñons, it is chiefly interesting for the ruined habitations of the Indians who once dwelt there. Dr. A. E. Douglass, director of Steward Observatory, University of Arizona, has studied the tree rings in the tough surviving timbers of the cliff dwellings, and by an ingenious matching of the beams to cover the different widths of rings for different years of rain and drought, he has determined that the masonry in Mug House, the earliest, dates back to 1066, the year that William the Conqueror became king of England. Cliff Palace was built, added to, and repaired from 1073 to 1273. Balcony House dates from 1190 to 1272; Spruce Tree House, 1230–1274.

The archeologists reveal for us a fascinating picture of the past. From the great mass of pottery and utensils rescued from the permanent dwellings of the Mesa Verde, the archeologists tell us that the second agricultural Basket Makers once lived in these ruins. By skeletons which have been found, they conclude that the long-headed Basket Makers were displaced, at least in part, by the round-headed Pueblos.

Visitors who climb about over the ruins of Cliff Palace, Balcony House, Square Tower House, and many others, may have the life of the one-time inhabitants reconstructed for them by the park guides. From the Park Service bulletin we may read: "The population was composed of a number of units, possibly clans, each of which had its more or less distinct social organization, as indicated in the arrangement of the rooms. The rooms occupied by a clan were not necessarily connected, and generally neighboring rooms were distinguished from one another by their uses. Thus, each clan had a room for its men, which is called the 'kiva.' Each clan had also a number of rooms which may be styled living rooms, and other enclosures for granaries. The corn was ground into meal in another room containing the metate set in a stone bin or trough. Sometimes the rooms had fireplaces, although these were generally in the plazas or on the housetops. All these different rooms, taken together, constituted the houses that belonged to one clan. . . . From the number of these rooms it would appear that there were at least 23 social units or clans in Cliff Palace. . . .

"In addition to their ability as architects and masons, the cliff dwellers excelled in the art of pottery making and as agriculturists. Their decorated pottery—a black design on pearly white background—will compare favorably with pottery of the other cultures of the prehistoric Southwest. . . . Their decoration of cotton fabrics and ceramic work might be called beautiful, even when judged by our own standards. They fashioned axes, spear points, and rude tools of stone; they wove sandals, and made attractive basketry."

The museum at Mesa Verde is one of the most entertaining in the United States. Artifacts in it, from the ruins, permit the daily lives of the cliff dwellers to be reconstructed.

Spruce Tree House, not far from the museum, is easy of access. Dr. J. Walter Fewkes, formerly chief of the Bureau of American Ethnology, was in charge of the excavation of most of the "houses" in the park. He found Spruce Tree House to be 216 feet long by 89 at its greatest width. He counted "eight ceremonial rooms, or kivas, and 114 rooms that had been used for living, storage and other purposes." Around the corner of the cliff there was a spring which furnished water. At one end of the cave, a trail of small toeholds in the face of the cliff was used by the men as they climbed to the mesa above, where corn, beans, and squash were raised. It is thought that the hunters also used the trail as they went in search of deer and mountain sheep.

Cliff Palace is larger, being 300 feet long, located in a spacious cave with a high arch just under the rim of the mesa floor and 200 feet above the canyon below. In Cliff Palace there are more than 200 living rooms, with twenty-two kivas in the cave.

The architecture of the cliff dwellers took advantage of the hanging caves prepared for them by wind and water erosion. On the firm rock base of the floor of the cave the women of the tribe built the walls of stone, crudely at first, but in the twelfth and thirteenth centuries with considerable masonry skill, introducing towers, three and four stories, constructing the floors and ceiling with strong tough timbers and crossing them with fine small timbers.

But all of the ruins are not found in the cliffs. There is Sun Temple, with its 1,000 feet of four-foot-thick walls and its complicated floor plan. There is Far View House, built on the level mesa, with its kiva thirty-two feet in diameter.

The park buildings were all built in the so-called Santa Fé type, under the direction of Jesse L. Nusbaum, who has done so much to interpret the Mesa Verde dwellings to the public.

SOUTHWESTERN NATIONAL MONUMENTS

A map of Arizona, New Mexico, and southern Utah and Colorado, dotted with the archeological parks and monuments and other remarkable features, would defy any simple routing. Frank Pinkley, Superintendent of the Southwestern Monuments lying in these four States, has figured out that a single trip to each, returning between trips to base at Coolidge, Arizona, would reach a mileage equal to a tour around the world on the circumference of the equator—and some of it would be equally hot! The Southwestern Monuments Association has recently (1939) issued "The Guide to Southwestern National Monuments," which locates and describes the twenty-six National Monuments administered from the Coolidge headquarters office. Unless one made a business of it, it would be impossible to visit all of these monuments on one trip. But it is possible to visit many of them on east-west trips. Three of these are in southern Utah. There are the forty-odd Arches, sculptured by wind erosion of red sandstone into unbelievably hospitable gateways; the tremendous Natural Bridge spans of solid sandstone, contrived on graceful supporting arches; and Rainbow Bridge of salmon-pink sandstone with a high arch "so nearly perfect" that "it dwarfs all human architecture" and so large that it could be arched over the Dome of the Capitol at Washington, with room to spare.

Across the Colorado-Utah line lies the Hovenweep National Monument, where are found "groups of remarkable prehistoric towers, pueblos, and cliff dwellings," built with a masonry so peculiar and specialized that, after centuries of exposure to the elements, parts of the ruins are in an excellent state of preservation. Not far from Mesa Verde in southwestern Colorado, the mounds of Yucca House cover ruins of buildings which once rose fifteen to twenty feet above the foundations and which were occupied in the "Classic Period." Southeast from Yucca House, across the New Mexico line, are the Aztec ruins, where there is a great E-shaped pueblo with 500 rooms and other pueblos yet uncovered.

Traveling east to west in northern New Mexico, not far from Raton, one arrives at Capulin Mountain National Monument —a "magnificent cinder cone" overlooking a region "which bears manifestations of tremendous volcanic activity."

On the road from Taos, a pueblo village occupied continuously for more than a thousand years, to Santa Fé, one may make a short detour to Bandelier National Monument, comprising Frijoles, Alamo, and other canyons. "The National Park Service highway and developments open up only about 300 acres in Frijoles Canyon on the edge of the area in order to make accessible famous 200-room Tyuonyi and other representative ruins. Hardy hikers or riders who seek the primeval can wander through some 25,000 acres of untouched wilderness and canyon country, seeing isolated Yapashi and other ruins." Most of Bandelier's ruins are of the Regressive Pueblo period, after the abandonment of the great pueblos and cliff dwellings of northwestern New Mexico.

West of Bandelier is Chaco Canyon National Monument, with "eighteen major and literally thousands of minor ruins." Pueblo Bonito "is one of the most imposing and best known ruins in the Southwest. Built more than one thousand years ago, this five-story, 800-room village was constructed in the shape of a great capital 'D' at the base of a cliff." Through tree-ring dating, archeologists have come to believe that the Chacoan towns were in ruins shortly after 1200 A. D., probably deserted because of droughts, possibly brought on by soil erosion and deforestation.

Still farther west, across the line in Arizona, is Canyon de

Photograph—Department of the Interior   Courtesy—Portfolio, American Planning and Civic Association

CARLSBAD CAVERNS NATIONAL PARK, NEW MEXICO

THE WHITE SANDS NATIONAL MONUMENT, NEW MEXICO
—A STRANGE SHIFTING BEAUTY

Photographs—Department of the Interior   Courtesy—Portfolio, American Planning and Civic Association

THE RUINS OF PUEBLO BONITO, CHACO CANYON, NEW MEXICO

MESA VERDE
NATIONAL PARK

TWO VIEWS OF
CLIFF PALACE

Photographs—Department of the Interior
Courtesy—American Planning and
Civic Annual, and Portfolio

BETATAKIN RUIN IN **NAVAJO** NATIONAL MONUMENT, ARIZONA

THE MIGHTY FALLEN TREES
OF THE PETRIFIED FOREST
NATIONAL MONUMENT

Photograph—Department of the Interior

Courtesy—Portfolio, American Planning
and Civic Association

CANYON DE CHELLY,
ARIZONA

Photograph—John W. Murray
Courtesy—Appalachia

[203]

A CLOSE-UP OF THE ANCIENT HABITATIONS OF
CANYON DE CHELLY, ARIZONA

MONTEZUMA CASTLE, ARIZONA—A PREHISTORIC RUIN

Artist James Russell; Photograph Rainbow Bridge-Monument Valley Expedition

AIR VIEW OVER MONUMENT VALLEY IN THE LAND OF THE NAVAJO

Chelly, but these ruins are not for the motorist who desires to keep on hard-surfaced roads and see his sights from a car window. "Within the boundaries of the monument lie more than a hundred miles of canyons of de Chelly and its two tributaries. . . . In shallow open-faced caves are found habitations ranging in time from a Basket Maker storage cist, whose roof beams dated 348 A. D. (the earliest accurately dated timber in the Southwest), to cliff dwellings abandoned in the thirteenth century."

Northwest of Canyon de Chelly, and inaccessible except in favorable weather, are the three "wonderful cliff dwellings" in "indescribably colorful and wild surroundings"—Keet Seel, Betatakin, and Inscription House. On the way south one may stop at Wupatki National Monument, where there are red sandstone prehistoric pueblos, "backgrounded by black basaltic cliffs and facing a view of the Painted Desert." Here 7,000 habitation sites have been discovered. Farther south is Sunset Crater, "most recent cone among the 400 others of the San Francisco volcanic field." South of the main highway is Walnut Canyon, twenty miles long and some 400 feet deep, occupied by some 300 cliff dwellings, proved by tree ringing to date from about 900 to 1200 A. D.

Not included under the administration of this group of monuments, but one, nevertheless, which every motorist should see, is the Petrified Forest between Gallup, New Mexico, and Holbrook, Arizona. Here lies a whole forest of petrified fallen giants.

Traveling south from Walnut Canyon one may visit Montezuma Castle, the best-preserved cliff dwelling in the United States. Built high in the cave of the cliff, the building is five stories high and contains 20 rooms within the walls proper. "Montezuma Castle probably was built during Pueblo III times (the period of great Pueblo advancement), and was occupied into the Regressive Period (Pueblo IV) after the great northern Pueblo centers were abandoned. It may have been constructed in part as early as 1100 A. D. and probably was deserted by 1425 A. D."

South of this is Tonto National Monument, where the cliff dwelling is situated on a cliff recess more than 300 feet above the headquarters area. Still farther south, at Coolidge, are the Casa Grande towers in "the largest of the six villages, to form by far the best preserved and most imposing ruin in the southern or Desert Province of the Southwest" named by Padre Kino in 1694. "Built of hard caliche clay with walls four feet thick at the base, Casa Grande was a watchtower-apartment house, for from its relatively great height its dwellers could watch for enemies."

Southeast of Casa Grande, almost down to the Mexican line, are the ruins of Tumacacori, one of Padre Kino's Sonora-Arizona chain of churches which, with San Xavier, were probably planned by two Italian brothers by the name of Gaona, architects.

In southern Arizona are two national monuments to preserve the native flora—the Saguaro, near Tucson, and the Organ Pipe Cactus on the Mexican border. In the southeastern corner of Arizona, near the New Mexico line, is the Chiricahua National Monument, where "weirdly eroded volcanic formations form a Wonderland of Rocks high atop the beautifully forested Chiricahua Mountains."

Traveling eastward into New Mexico one finds the White Sands National Monument, where "glistening white gypsum and sand dunes, ten to sixty feet high, cover 500 square miles of the Tularoa Basin." North, near the center of New Mexico, in the Gran Quivira, we find the "new" church of the Spanish padres, begun in 1649, never completely finished, but still lifting its massive walls forty feet in the air. Northwest of this is El Morro, "a great buff promontory, rising 200 feet above the surrounding lava-strewn valley," resembling a huge castle or fortress. The Spaniards named it and left inscriptions on it, the earliest dated 1605 (or 1606), and the latest 1774. But the Spaniards were not the first to find the rock, with its cove and pool of water, "for high on the easily fortified mesa top are large ruins of pueblos which were built during Pueblo IV, the Regressive Pueblo Period, in the neighborhood of 1400 A. D. These peoples engraved undecipherable symbols on the rock, so El Morro's records cover more than 500 years."

In the wilderness of the Mogollon Mountains of western New Mexico are the Gila cliff dwellings, more interesting for their surroundings than for any special distinction.

These Southwestern Monuments preserve some of the most important geological, archeological, and historical evidences of the past forces and civilizations of the region. No traveler can claim to have seen the Southwest who has not visited some of them.

EAST OF THE MISSISSIPPI

THE MYSTERIOUS APPALACHIANS

THE APPALACHIAN TRAIL

PERHAPS the best introduction to the eastern mountain wilderness is The Appalachian Trail, which was first proposed by Benton MacKaye in 1921, and which has been realized since by the use of existing trails and the building and maintenance of new trails and feeders by the mountain and trail clubs along the way. "Mr. MacKaye," wrote Myron Avery in *American Forests*, "conceived the plan of a trail which, for all practical purposes, should be endless. He regarded it as the backbone of a primeval environment, a sort of retreat or refuge from a civilization which was becoming too mechanized." The trail starts at Mt. Katahdin, "a massive granite monolith in the central Maine wilderness," and runs for a distance of 2,050 miles south to Mt. Oglethorpe, in northern Georgia. Only part of Mt. Katahdin is in public ownership, but it is hoped that the entire mountain where the wilderness trail begins can be made a park, and the surrounding forests, insofar as they have been injured, allowed to revert to their previous wild condition.

The trail touches Grafton Notch, the White and Green Mountains, Mt. Greylock, Mohawk and Bear Mountains, Delaware Water Gap, and South Mountain before it reaches Shenandoah National Park.

SHENANDOAH

The Shenandoah National Park preserves the crest of the Blue Ridge Mountains, a part of the Appalachian system in Virginia between the Piedmont Plateau and the Shenandoah Valley, extending from Front Royal almost to Waynesboro, a distance of nearly a hundred miles. Though there is a Skyline Drive along most of the crest of the park, in most places the Appalachian Trail is well removed from the highway. Those who hike over the main and side trails of the Shenandoah Park are usually surprised at the feeling of remoteness and at the wilderness charm of much of the region. The Hawksbill, Old Rag, and other trails lead into rough country, and will remain among the favorite hikes of the Potomac Appalachian Trail Club. President Hoover's Rapidan Camp, which the Federal Government received by gift, is within the park.

There were different schools of thought concerning the Skyline Drive. Many of the hikers thought that the few old "horse-and-buggy" dirt access roads, unsuitable for automobiles, should never have been replaced by improved access and crest-line highways. It should be remembered, however, that at best Shenandoah Park is a narrow strip, flanked closely by inhabited valleys, so that, highway or no highway, the sense of remoteness is due to favorable topography, which provides an illusion of distance where there is no great distance. The rugged crests, the finely timbered valleys, and the plashing of waterfalls contribute to that sense of isolation, though all the time there are nearby habitations. The land belonging to the mountaineer settlers within the park has been purchased and allowed to revert to wilderness.

There are stretches of the Skyline Drive which give to the motorist some of the wilderness aspects. There are places where, from a car window, one may see in the misty distance crest on crest of mountain spurs, with no glimpse of the busy towns so near in the valleys below. At other outlooks the view includes the smoke of scores of towns, picturesque enough, as seen from the mountain tops. Many of those familiar with the principal western parks have commented enthusiastically on the great beauty of the Blue Ridge Mountains as seen from the Skyline Drive. It must be admitted that there are some lovely spots on the drive which were once much prized by hikers and which are now so near the highway that they have lost most of their charm, but The Appalachian Trail in the park is really very well located, and its users are little bothered by the highway, which, after all, gives them easy access to the forested valleys and high peaks. Considering the narrowness of the park, it is rather a miracle that both the highway and the trail interfere so little.

In the spring when the dogwood scallops with frothy white embroidery the edges of the spruce and hemlock forests, and later, when the dainty dimity pink of the laurel stitches in its rosy note of color, the Shenandoah is very lovely. Every year there are countless trips to see the beds of modest trilliums, white and pink

Photograph—Department of the Interior   Courtesy—Portfolio, American Planning and Civic Association

MT. KATAHDIN, MAINE (ABOVE) BEGINS THE APPALACHIAN TRAIL

CHIMNEY ON ARMADILLO   GREEN SLAB

Photographs—M. B. Howarth   Courtesy—Appalachia

Photograph—George Knox

LOOKING TOWARD HAWKSBILL IN THE SHENANDOAH
NATIONAL PARK

and painted. From the time when the trailing arbutus puts out its delicate fairy cups and the yellow lady's slipper hangs its charming blossoms on the green of the forest floor, through the weeks of the brilliant red-bud, the pink and white azaleas, the more showy rhododendrons, to the October days when the hardwood forests are painted bright red and yellow and brown in a glorious riot of color, the Shenandoah provides for thousands of those who live in nearby Atlantic seaboard cities, the peace and recreation which come from forest, mountain, and stream. As the park is becoming known, visitors come to it from all parts of the United States.

GREAT SMOKY MOUNTAINS

Ever since the days when Charles Egbert Craddock captured the imagination of the American people with her novel, "The Prophet of the Great Smoky Mountains," the curling mists of the Smokies, which look so much like rising wreaths of smoke, have cast a spell of enchantment over those who looked from the valleys of North Carolina and Tennessee into these mysterious mountains.

When the five hundred miles of the Blue Ridge Parkway are completed, one will be able to drive the length of the Shenandoah from Front Royal on through Virginia, and by a spreading fork enter the Great Smoky Mountains National Park from the east or the west, then crossing the Divide at Newfound Gap, from which a spur runs out to Clingmans Dome.

There are about seventy-five miles of The Appalachian Trail in the Great Smoky Mountains National Park, traversing Old Black, Guyot, Chapman, Laurel Top, Kephart, Clingmans Dome, Silers Bald, Thunderhead, and Gregory and Parsons Balds. In the northern part of the park the forests are dense spruce and fir, but in the southern part there are hardwood forests and many mountains bald of any forest cover. Carlos Campbell, in *American Forests*, gave an excellent account of an eight-day hike which covered the trail within the Smoky Mountains, "the roughest and highest portion of the entire Appalachian Trail." The crest of the Great Smokies for thirty-six miles in the park is more than 5,000 feet in altitude, with sixteen peaks above 6,000 feet high.

This park gives us our largest wilderness area in the East. The rugged mountain crests, the virgin spruce, the fine variety of hardwoods, and the heavy rainfall which produces a rich forest floor, give to the Smokies a tropical luxuriance not found in any other mountain region in the United States, with the possible exception of the Olympics. There are in the park 129 native tree species and twenty varieties of large shrubs. Tourists come from afar to see the rhododendrons bloom in June. On a single trip up the mountain, at different levels mountain laurel, flame azaleas, and rhododendrons may be seen in their full glory. The native flower gardens of the Smokies, though quite different from the western types, rival them in color and growth.

Six hundred miles of trout streams are in the park. There are 56 miles of high-grade roads, 25 miles of secondary roads, 165 miles of truck trails (not public), and 510 miles of horse and foot trails.

On the top of Mt. LeConte there is a lodge to which all supplies are taken on pack animals. The sunrise and sunset views from Myrtle Point and other vantage lookouts are magnificent, and well repay the 5,000-foot climb from Gatlinburg to the mountain top. Accommodations may be found outside the park at Gatlinburg, Tennessee, near the park line, and in North Carolina towns somewhat farther from the park.

WHERE LAND AND WATER MEET

One established park and three authorized projects of "water-front" national parks lie east of the Mississippi.

ACADIA

Far north on the coast of Maine, in what was once French territory, Acadia National Park preserves the Mt. Desert Mountains, "whose ancient uplift, worn by immeasurable time and recent ice erosion, remains to form the largest rock-built island on our Atlantic coast, 'l'Isle des Monts deserts,' as Champlain named it." As early as 1855 summer visitors began to come to Mt. Desert Island, because of its beauty and cool summer climate. In 1914, 5,000 acres of the island were offered to the National Government by the Hancock County Trustees of Public

Reservations, and in 1916 President Wilson proclaimed the area to be the Sieur de Monts National Monument. In 1919, by Act of Congress, the area was included in the Lafayette National Park, and ten years later, when the park was enlarged, its name was changed to Acadia. George B. Dorr has given lands, money, and watchful oversight to Acadia, where he has served as superintendent and host for many years.

The native growth of the Acadian forest has, for the most part, escaped fires and human destruction. There are many varieties of pine and spruce, balsam firs, larches and arborvitae among the conifers, and a wide selection among the hardwoods.

But the great appeal of Acadia lies in the high, rocky cliffs and the beating surf of the Atlantic Ocean. From the mountain tops and from many vantage points along the driveway up Cadillac Mountain one may look out over the deep blue waters, with the many wooded and rocky promontories. The auto caravans, with ranger naturalists in charge, are very popular in this park, as are also the sea cruises around Frenchman Bay. In addition to the motor roads, there are some fifty miles of roads restricted to the use of saddle and driving horses, and this gives a taste of the age before the advent of automobiles. There are 150 miles of trails and footpaths—charming walks all, with many fine views. Accommodations are to be found outside the park in the various villages. The park headquarters are at Bar Harbor.

ISLE ROYALE, LAKE SUPERIOR

Lying just below the international water boundary in Lake Superior is Isle Royale, the largest island in the lake. Through Acts of Congress, dating from 1931, the Federal Government has indicated its desire to accept Isle Royale as a national park.

The picturesque rocky shore-line reminds one of Acadia National Park, and when Lake Superior rages in storm, the breaking surf completes the simile. The rolling hills and bare granite ledges are softened in the hazy summer air, and in the scrubby forests and on the shores of the numerous little lakes are found moose, coyotes, beaver, and other forest animals. In the waters are famous lake trout, whitefish, and muskellunge or pike.

Those who have been traveling by boat to this distant island for their summer vacations report that they acquire here a feeling of remoteness and peacefulness which seems to be one of the psychological tests for national-park fitness, along with other qualifications of land and water resources.

HATTERAS

On August 17, 1937, Congress authorized the acceptance of the first National Seashore, to cover historic Cape Hatteras and its lighthouse off the coast of North Carolina, covering roughly 100 square miles on the islands of Chicamacomico, Ocracoke, Bodie, Roanoke, and Collington. H. E. Weatherwax, writing in *Landscape Architecture*, makes the claim that "The North Carolina banks offer the finest type of Atlantic seacoast country. The area has never been developed, and its glistening beaches extend uninterrupted for miles. The series of barrier islands, or bars, on which the national seashore will be established were built of sand washed up from the sea and distributed by longshore currents. The foundations of the barrier were laid during the last stages of the ice age, when so much water was locked in the polar ice sheets that the level of the sea was 25 feet or more lower than at present. The beach ridge formed at that time is thought to have produced islands or shoals when the sea was raised to its present level by the melting of the ice. These were converted into the existing barrier formations by wave action."

EVERGLADES

On the southwest end of the peninsula in Florida, extending south of any other continental territory of the United States, we have the Everglades—a water-logged wilderness of twisted mangroves, penetrated by a complicated maze of water channels which may be navigated by boats. The whole region is rich in tropical bird life—blue herons, white egrets and ibises, brilliant red flamingoes, filling the air with their cloudy flights and perching on limbs of trees like so many huge blossoms. The Everglades, authorized to be accepted by the Federal Government as a gift, will one day be one of the most unique parks in the system. But haste is needed if the disastrous effects of forest fires and the predatory operations of the bird killers are to be circumvented.

IN GREAT SMOKY MOUNTAINS NATIONAL PARK

CREST OF THE
GREAT SMOKY MOUNTAINS
NATIONAL PARK

Courtesy—American Civic Annual

FALLS ON ROARING FORK CREEK—ONE OF EIGHT BETWEEN THE BLUFF
AND THE TOP OF MT. LECONTE. GREAT SMOKY MOUNTAINS NATIONAL PARK

Photograph—Thompson, Inc.   Courtesy—American Forests

Photograph—Department of the Interior

Courtesy—Portfolio, American Planning and Civic Association

RHODODENDRONS IN GREAT SMOKY MOUNTAINS NATIONAL PARK

Photograph—George Masa Courtesy—Portfolio, American Planning and Civic Association

VIRGIN HARDWOODS
IN GREAT SMOKY MOUNTAINS NATIONAL PARK

TRAIL ON TOP OF
CADILLAC MOUNTAIN

Courtesy — Portfolio, American
Planning and Civic Association

ACADIA
NATIONAL PARK

THE THUNDERHOLE

Photographs—Department of
the Interior

Courtesy—Landscape Architecture

[221]

MOOSE IN ISLE ROYALE, LAKE SUPERIOR

THE SHIFTING SANDS AND WIND-BLOWN TREES
CAPE HATTERAS SEASHORE

Photographs—Department of the Interior   Courtesy—Landscape Architecture

PROPOSED EVERGLADES
NATIONAL PARK

CONGRESS HAS AUTHORIZED THE DE-
PARTMENT OF THE INTERIOR TO ACCEPT
THE FLORIDA EVERGLADES AS A
NATIONAL PARK WHEN ALL PRIVATE
LANDS HAVE BEEN ACQUIRED AND THE
REGION DONATED TO THE FEDERAL
GOVERNMENT. THE WHITE IBISES GIVE
A TROPICAL BEAUTY TO THESE
PICTURESQUE EVERGLADES

Photographs—Matlack Studio

Courtesy—Portfolio, American Planning
and Civic Association

WAKEFIELD, THE RESTORED BIRTHPLACE OF GEORGE WASHINGTON

IN COLONIAL VIRGINIA

Photographs—Department of the Interior

Courtesy—American Planning and Civic Annual

THE MOORE HOUSE AT YORKTOWN

Photograph—Virginia State Chamber of Commerce   Courtesy—Portfolio, American Planning and Civic Association

A QUIET STREET IN OLD YORKTOWN, WHERE THERE IS A
COLONIAL NATIONAL HISTORICAL PARK

Photographs—Department of the Interior   Courtesy—Portfolio, American Planning and Civic Association

JAMESTOWN ISLAND, WHERE THE EXCAVATION OF SEVENTEENTH-
CENTURY FOUNDATIONS HAS REVEALED VALUABLE EVIDENCE OF
THE LIFE OF THE EARLY SETTLERS ON THE ATLANTIC SEABOARD

IN MORRISTOWN NATIONAL
HISTORICAL PARK

THE FORD MANSION SERVED AS
WASHINGTON'S HEADQUARTERS
DURING THE WINTER OF 1779–
1780. THE HOUSE IS NOW OPEN
TO THE PUBLIC.

Photographs—Department of the Interior
Courtesy—Portfolio, American Planning
and Civic Association

NATIONAL HISTORICAL PARKS AND MONUMENTS

The Colonial National Historical Park, authorized by the Cramton Act of 1930, sets aside Jamestown Island, the site of the first permanent English settlement in North America; parts of the city of Williamsburg (privately owned and restored by funds furnished by Mr. John D. Rockefeller, Jr.); and Yorktown, where in 1781 the French and Americans besieged and captured the Army of Cornwallis in the last important battle of the Revolution.

No one who visits this cradle of American liberties can fail to be thrilled with the quaintness of quiet old Yorktown, where it is said there was established the first Custom House on American soil. The atmosphere of past centuries still hangs over this Virginia village, and many of the famous houses of Colonial times are still standing in gardens where the present-day paths follow the lines of the garden makers of the eighteenth century. In Yorktown there are museums to interpret the story, and many of the siege fortification features have been restored and the artillery emplacements reinstalled.

There is a charming parkway skirting the beautiful York River, which connects Yorktown and Williamsburg, where Mr. Rockefeller's restoration presents the old capital city, along lines discovered to be authentic through the study of old records. Today one may see the heart of Williamsburg very much as it was in Colonial times. The Duke of Gloucester Street extends from the rebuilt Capitol to the College of William and Mary, with its old and new buildings. From the Old Bruton Parish Church a cross axis approaches by a parked highway the Governor's Palace, set amid an elaborate garden of English box and flowers. Along the main street are many restored homes and the rebuilt Raleigh Tavern, where so many important historic events took place. As the restorations take on the patina of age, there will live here again the scene of old Williamsburg, an atmosphere which is fostered by the Colonial costumes worn by the guides.

On Jamestown Island, which will one day be the western terminus of the Yorktown Parkway, the excavations of the eighteenth-century foundations have brought to light more than 80,000 pottery fragments, some 75,000 glass fragments, 85,000 iron and nearly 50,000 clay-pipe fragments, which, when studied, will help us to reconstruct the daily lives of our earliest forebears on the Atlantic seaboard.

The second National Historical Park to be created was established in 1933 in New Jersey. Morristown Park preserves sites of important military encampments during the Revolution, the Ford Mansion, which served as Washington's headquarters during the crucial winter of 1779–80, other eighteenth-century houses, a museum and a collection of Washingtoniana.

Though these two parks are the only ones to be named officially National Historical Parks, there has developed a well-defined historical program in the National Park Service. From the time of its establishment in 1916, there have been included in the system areas of archeological and historical interest. From eight in 1916, these have grown to more than 100 in 1938. By the Act of August 21, 1935, Congress declared it to be a national policy to preserve historic and archeological sites of national significance for the pleasure and benefit of the people. The Secretary of the Interior was granted broad powers intended to place upon the National Park Service responsibility for leadership in a renewed nation-wide movement to conserve our remaining unprotected historic and archeological treasures. As a part of this program, the Historic American Buildings Survey was initiated by the National Park Service, and includes among its accomplishments a permanent working agreement with the Fine Arts Division of the Library of Congress and the American Institute of Architects to measure and record the irreplaceable architecture of the American past.

The American Antiquities Act of 1906, the Historic and Archeological Act of 1935, the appointment by the Secretary of the Interior of the Advisory Board of National Parks, Historic Sites, Buildings, and Monuments, of which Dr. Hermon C. Bumpus is chairman, and of the National Advisory Committee of the Historic American Buildings Survey, of which Dr. Leicester B. Holland is chairman, together with the transfer by President Franklin D. Roosevelt in 1933 of all National Monuments to the National Park Service, have conspired to develop a consistent program.

Among many National Military Parks transferred were those of Chickamauga, Missionary Ridge, and Lookout Mountain, near Chattanooga, Tennessee; six great Civil War battlefields, near

Fredericksburg in Virginia, Gettysburg in Pennsylvania, Shiloh in Tennessee, and Vicksburg in Mississippi. The Park Service is preserving also such Historical Monuments in Florida as Fort Jefferson, largest all-masonry fortification in the Western World, built in 1846 for control of the Florida Straits, which served as a military prison during the Civil War; Fort Marion, oldest fort extant in the United States, originally Castle San Marcos, constructed of coquina by the Spanish to defend their Florida possessions; and Fort Mantanzas, an early Spanish stronghold.

When the Spanish Monuments in California and the Southwest are considered with those of Florida, it may readily be seen that, through the preservation of historic sites, the entire Spanish northern frontier which extended in a long three-thousand-mile arc from California to Florida, may be visualized and studied by students of history. When the fine archeological monuments of the Southwest are considered with such monuments as Ocmulgee in Georgia, which preserves an area near Macon, "containing the most unique and important Indian mounds in the Southeast, the excavation of which has thrown new light on the pre-Columbian Indian civilization," the possibilities of extensive archeological research in the known and yet-to-be-discovered prehistoric ruins seem unlimited. Here is a treasure house of source material for the study of American history, useful for research and for demonstration.

In the East, the first National Parkways have been developed. The George Washington Memorial Parkway from Mount Vernon, through Alexandria, to the Arlington Memorial Bridge leading into Washington, and now being extended to the Great Falls of the Potomac in Virginia, was the first to be undertaken in 1930. The Blue Ridge Parkway, already mentioned as connecting Shenandoah and Great Smoky Mountains National Parks, is now under construction, and the Colonial Parkway between Williamsburg and Yorktown is already in use. The Natchez Trace Parkway, authorized in 1934 and 1938, to follow the general location of the famous old Indian Trail between Nashville and Natchez, is now being surveyed.

Probably most of the national parks will one day be connected by parkways, with sufficient rights-of-way to protect the eyes of those who drive over them from any sort of objectionable encroachment, and making the most of the natural roadside scenery.

The National Park Service fell heir in 1933 to the park system of the Federal City, which, under the name District of Columbia, was first established by Act of Congress, approved July 16, 1790, and which has been under continuous Federal control ever since. There are nearly 7,500 acres in the system, covering more than 700 areas and about 75 national statues and memorials, among which are the Washington Monument and the Lincoln Memorial in Washington and the Lee Mansion, across the Potomac River in Arlington. C. Marshall Finnan, formerly superintendent of Mesa Verde National Park, presides over the regional park system of the Nation's Capital.

The entire eastern part of the United States is marked with statues of historic significance, with battlefields, with historic sites and buildings, with cemeteries in which lie the famous dead of our early history. Those who travel by motor, with the aid of the National Park Service may seek out as many of these historic reminders of the past as they have time to cover. This is a fascinating way to study the history of the United States.

One National Monument there is, last seen by every departing ocean passenger from the port of New York, and hailed by every returning patriot, who may see in it that pledge of individual independence from government oppression which it was meant to commemorate—the Statue of Liberty, holding high the lighted torch of liberal leadership, given by the French Government to the American people as visible evidence to the world of the French alliance which helped to establish the Republic of the United States of America.

THE STATUE OF LIBERTY—A NATIONAL MONUMENT

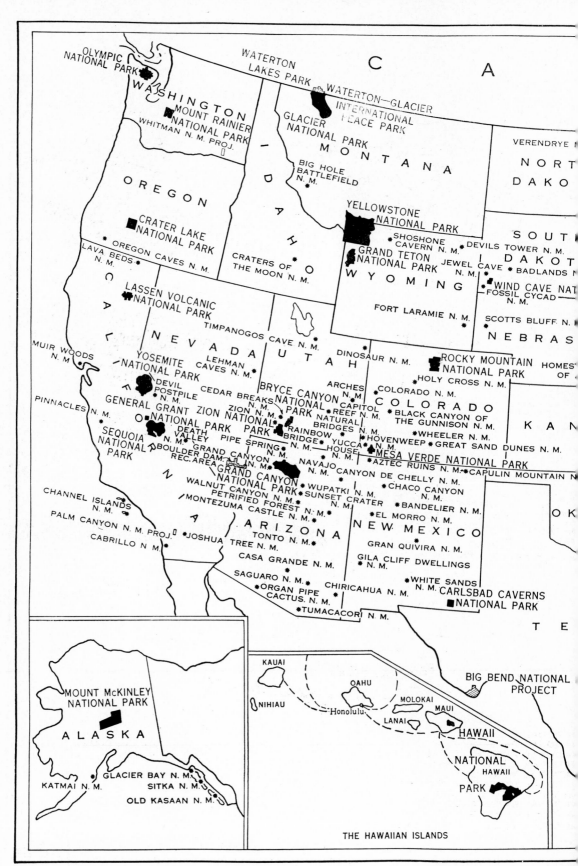

OLYMPIC
NATIONAL PARK

WASHINGTON

MOUNT RAINIER
NATIONAL PARK
WHITMAN N. M. PROJ.

C A

WATERTON
LAKES PARK   WATERTON—GLACIER
INTERNATIONAL
PEACE PARK

GLACIER
NATIONAL PARK

MONTANA

VERENDRYE N

NORT

DAKO

OREGON

CRATER LAKE
NATIONAL PARK

OREGON CAVES N. M.

LAVA BEDS
N. M.

BIG HOLE
BATTLEFIELD
N. M.

I D A H O

CRATERS OF
THE MOON N. M.

YELLOWSTONE
NATIONAL PARK

SHOSHONE
CAVERN N. M.

GRAND TETON
NATIONAL PARK

WYOMING

FORT LARAMIE N. M.

DEVILS TOWER N. M.

JEWEL CAVE
N. M.

WIND CAVE NAT
FOSSIL CYCAD
N. M.

SCOTTS BLUFF N.

SOUT

DAKOT

BADLANDS N

NEBRAS

LASSEN VOLCANIC
NATIONAL PARK

N E V A D A

TIMPANOGOS CAVE N. M.

LEHMAN
CAVES N. M.

U T A H

DINOSAUR N. M.

ROCKY MOUNTAIN
NATIONAL PARK

HOLY CROSS N. M.

HOMES
OF

MUIR WOODS
N. M.

YOSEMITE
NATIONAL PARK

C A L

PINNACLES N. M.

DEVIL
POSTPILE
N. M.

GENERAL GRANT
NATIONAL PARK

SEQUOIA
NATIONAL
PARK

CHANNEL ISLANDS
N. M.

PALM CANYON N. M. PROJ.

CABRILLO N. M.

CEDAR BREAKS
N. M.

ZION NATIONAL
PARK

ZION
N. M.

DEATH
VALLEY
N. M.

BOULDER DAM
REC. AREA

GRAND CANYON
N. M.

GRAND CANYON
NATIONAL PARK

WALNUT
CANYON N. M.

PETRIFIED FOREST N. M.

MONTEZUMA CASTLE N. M.

JOSHUA TREE N. M.

A R I Z O N A

TONTO N. M.

CASA GRANDE N. M.

SAGUARO N. M.

ORGAN PIPE
CACTUS. N. M.

BRYCE CANYON
NATIONAL
PARK

CAPITOL
REEF N. M.

NATURAL
BRIDGES N. M.

RAINBOW
BRIDGE
N. M.

PIPE SPRING
N. M.

RAINBOW
HOUSE

YUCCA
N. M.

NAVAJO
N. M.

CANYON DE CHELLY N. M.

WUPATKI N. M.

SUNSET CRATER
N. M.

ARCHES
N. M.

COLORADO N. M.

BLACK CANYON OF
THE GUNNISON N. M.

HOVENWEEP
N. M.

WHEELER N. M.

MESA VERDE NATIONAL PARK

AZTEC RUINS N. M.

CHACO CANYON
N. M.

BANDELIER N. M.

EL MORRO N. M.

C O L O R A D O

GREAT SAND DUNES N. M.

CAPULIN MOUNTAIN N

N E W   M E X I C O

GRAN QUIVIRA N. M.

GILA CLIFF DWELLINGS
N. M.

WHITE SANDS
N. M.

CHIRICAHUA N. M.

TUMACACORI N. M.

CARLSBAD CAVERNS
NATIONAL PARK

K A N

OK

T E

NATIONAL PARK SERV

MOUNT McKINLEY
NATIONAL PARK

A L A S K A

KATMAI N. M.

GLACIER BAY N. M.

SITKA N. M.

OLD KASAAN N. M.

KAUAI

NIHIAU

OAHU

Honolulu

MOLOKAI

LANAI

MAUI

BIG BEND NATIONAL
PROJECT

HAWAII

NATIONAL

HAWAII

PARK

THE HAWAIIAN ISLANDS

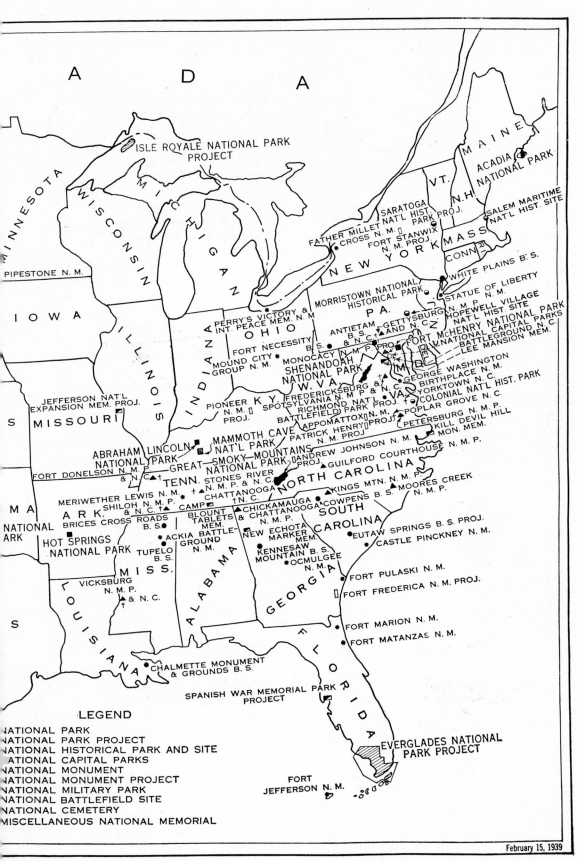

ISLE ROYALE NATIONAL PARK PROJECT

A   D   A

MAINE

ACADIA NATIONAL PARK

SALEM MARITIME NAT'L HIST. SITE

VT.

N.H.

MINNESOTA

WISCONSIN

MICHIGAN

SARATOGA NAT'L HIST. PARK PROJ.

FATHER MILLET CROSS N.M.

FORT STANWIX N.M. PROJ.

NEW YORK

MASS.

CONN.

WHITE PLAINS B.S.

STATUE OF LIBERTY N.M.

MORRISTOWN NATIONAL HISTORICAL PARK

HOPEWELL VILLAGE NAT'L HIST. SITE

PA.

PIPESTONE N.M.

IOWA

PERRY'S VICTORY & INT. PEACE MEM. N.M

OHIO

GETTYSBURG N.M.P. AND N.C.

FORT McHENRY NATIONAL PARK

ANTIETAM B.S. & N.C.

NATIONAL CAPITAL PARKS

BATTLEGROUND N.C.

LEE MANSION MEM.

FORT NECESSITY B.S.

INDIANA

MOUND CITY GROUP N.M.

MONOCACY N.M.P. PROJ.

SHENANDOAH NATIONAL PARK

W. VA.

MD.

GEORGE WASHINGTON BIRTHPLACE N.M.

JEFFERSON NAT'L EXPANSION MEM. PROJ.

PIONEER N.M. PROJ.

KY.

FREDERICKSBURG & SPOTSYLVANIA N.M.P. & N.C.

RICHMOND NATL BATTLEFIELD PARK PROJ.

VA.

YORKTOWN N.C.

COLONIAL NAT'L HIST. PARK

MISSOURI

ILLINOIS

APPOMATTOX N.M.

PATRICK HENRY N.M. PROJ.

POPLAR GROVE N.C.

PETERSBURG N.M.P.

ABRAHAM LINCOLN NATIONAL PARK

MAMMOTH CAVE NAT'L PARK

KILL DEVIL HILL MON. MEM.

FORT DONELSON N.M.P. & N.C.

GREAT SMOKY MOUNTAINS NATIONAL PARK

ANDREW JOHNSON N.M. PROJ.

GUILFORD COURTHOUSE N.M.P.

NORTH CAROLINA

TENN.

STONES RIVER N.M.P. & N.C.

KINGS MTN. N.M.P.

MOORES CREEK N.M.P.

MERIWETHER LEWIS N.M.

CHATTANOOGA N.C.

COWPENS B.S.

ARK.

SHILOH N.M.P. & N.C.

CAMP

CHICKAMAUGA & CHATTANOOGA N.M.P.

SOUTH

BRICES CROSS ROADS B.S.

BLOUNT TABLETS MEM.

NEW ECHOTA MARKER MEM.

CAROLINA

EUTAW SPRINGS B.S. PROJ.

CASTLE PINCKNEY N.M.

HOT SPRINGS NATIONAL PARK

MA.

NATIONAL ARK

ACKIA BATTLE-GROUND N.M.

TUPELO B.S.

KENNESAW MOUNTAIN B.S.

OCMULGEE N.M.

MISS.

GEORGIA

FORT PULASKI N.M.

VICKSBURG N.M.P.

& N.C.

ALABAMA

FORT FREDERICA N.M. PROJ.

LOUISIANA

FLORIDA

FORT MARION N.M.

FORT MATANZAS N.M.

CHALMETTE MONUMENT & GROUNDS B.S.

SPANISH WAR MEMORIAL PARK PROJECT

EVERGLADES NATIONAL PARK PROJECT

FORT JEFFERSON N.M.

LEGEND

NATIONAL PARK
NATIONAL PARK PROJECT
NATIONAL HISTORICAL PARK AND SITE
NATIONAL CAPITAL PARKS
NATIONAL MONUMENT
NATIONAL MONUMENT PROJECT
NATIONAL MILITARY PARK
NATIONAL BATTLEFIELD SITE
NATIONAL CEMETERY
MISCELLANEOUS NATIONAL MEMORIAL

February 15, 1939

AREAS AND PROJECTS

Photograph -- Department of the Interior

Courtesy—Portfolio, American Planning and Civic Association

THE NATIONAL PARKS ARE THE HIKERS' PARADISE

RETROSPECT

Looking backward over our journeys in the National Parks and Monuments, we can hardly forget that great elation of spirit which crowned our views of untamed natural beauty—that mastery of ego and transcendence of self which found us high on the mountain tops. We came face to face with the mighty living glaciers which are still grinding away at their assigned task. We took to heart the thought that the stars in their courses have achieved a speed and direction which make man-made aircraft seem like silly children's toys. We marveled at the ingenuity of Nature in fashioning mountains, valleys, and streams, in husbanding forests, shrubs, and flowers, with their infinite variety of form and color. We thanked "whatever gods there be" for the birds and the beasts that we had seen, for it would be a sorry, silent world if mankind were here alone.

All that we had read of geology was illustrated with dramatic dioramas on a ten-league canvas. We felt that we had torn aside the curtain of Time and looked into the daily lives of those early Indians who lived high in the cliffs in the year 1000. We had looked upon the buildings of the Spanish padres and the scenes of the early explorers. In the East we had visited the Colonial villages where our early history was made. We had looked upon the battlefields where hard-won victories have made possible our present-day Nation. We had entered the houses where the great leaders of our country were born or lived.

When the National Park and Monument System is completed, as it will be during the next few years, the United States of America will own a rich landed estate in which may be preserved those tangible and intangible values that can never be completely enjoyed when combined with the economic exploitation of our land and water resources.

Perhaps in the soul-satisfying beauties of our national parks and other sacred regions we shall find that we can regain something of that poise of outlook and courage in action which contact with unspoiled Nature may confer on human beings, and so ensure a continuance of our civilization on the lands which were so lately conquered by our ancestors.

Let us cherish the domain we have received from the hands of Nature, and in using it for our collective enjoyment manage it wisely and damage it as little as possible. Let us study the pages of its story. Let us sense its romance. And finally, let us receive its benediction!

INDEX

INDEX